"AMERICA GOES CHICKEN CRAZY"

"Soon, chicken, not beef, could be America's No. 1 meat."

N.R. Kleinfield. *New York Times*

ALSO EDITED BY BARBARA S. ROSENBERG

- IN THE BEGINNING, A Collection of Hors d'Oeuvres

- BEGINNING AGAIN — More Hors d'Oeuvres

- CINCINNATI ZOOSTERS' COOKIE AND BREAD RECIPES

- LOW CHOLESTEROL GOURMET CUISINE

Member of

International Association of Cooking Schools

HOW TO SUCCEED WITH CHICKEN
WITHOUT EVEN FRYING

By

BARBARA S. ROSENBERG

edited by

FRANCES ROSENBERG HENDRICK

Illustrated by
ALICE H. BALTERMAN

MarLance, Inc.
Books for Cooks

1070 Barry Lane
Cincinnati, Ohio 45229
(513) 281-0530 / 791-8452

1st Printing — November, 1984

HOW TO SUCCEED WITH CHICKEN WITHOUT EVEN FRYING

Library of Congress Cataloguing in Publication Data

Main entry under title:

How to Succeed With Chicken Without Even Frying

Includes index.
1. Cookery   2. Menus
84-090615

Printed by
The Feicke Printing Co.
Cincinnati, Ohio

Typeset by
Reporter Typographics
Cincinnati, Ohio

ISBN 0-9613733-7-7

To our families who never chickened out!

And to our artist and advisor,
Alice Balterman.
Her perceptiveness and fine sense of humor translated
our concept of sophisticated whimsy into reality.

Special thanks to dear friends for their gracious help, their
enthusiasm, and their confidence.
Peggy Barrett
Ruth Coppel
Adelaide Cunningham
Lois Friedman
Rebecca Horner
Joan Schaengold

The authors gratefully acknowledge permission to reprint from the following:
Beginning Again, More Hors d'Oeuvres. Copyright © 1981 by Rockdale Ridge Press.

How to Buy Economically, A Food Buyer's Guide. 1981 by the United States Department of Agriculture Food Safety and Quality Service.

In The Beginning, A Collection of Hors d'Oeuvres. Copyright © 1975 by Rockdale Ridge Press.

Publications of the National Broiler Council.

Publications of the Consumers Products Division of Reynolds Aluminum.

Serpico by Peter Maas. Copyright © 1973 by Peter Maas and Tsampa Co. Reprinted by permission of Viking Penguin, Inc.

FOREWORD

How To Succeed With Chicken Without Even Frying is a book for the present. Chicken recipes are in universal demand. As today's most recommended meat, chicken is economical in terms of money, calories, cholesterol, and preparation time. Herein lie recipes and features to meet the needs of every chef. There are elegant menus for the Saturday night chef, homestyle menus and tips on economizing for the chef with a family, and instructions for partially preparing meals in advance for the working chef. For the beginning chef, we have written step-by-step instructions and a complete reference chapter. You will find original family favorites as well as traditional recipes adapted for today's busy chef.

In keeping with the trend toward lowered fat consumption, we frequently accomplish the crisping of the chicken skin by broiling, then draining excess fat, rather than by the standard method of frying. This *reduces* the total fat consumed instead of increasing it as in the frying method. A full set of instructions for the cholesterol-conscious chef appears on **page 179.**

Time is at a premium in today's fast-paced lifestyle. We have carefully streamlined our menus so that even with a minimum of time, you, our reader, can prepare a lovely, inviting meal. There is no time wasted trying to decide what to make; menus do the thinking *for* you. There is no time wasted on preliminaries; by following the simple instructions in "Nest Eggs," you will have the necessary staples at your fingertips. (We're so serious about that, that we have included labels.) With the brief instructions at the bottom of each recipe, you can prepare much of the menu in advance. And there's no need to be buried in dishes at the end; our recipes make extensive use of flameproof serving dishes and cooking bags to minimize clean-up.

Chicken sets the stage to show off any favorite ingredient; it is chameleon-like in its ability to take on the character of the vegetable, fruit, or sauce with which it is prepared. And it is those accenting ingredients which propel chicken from a Sandwich Bar to a Candlelight Dinner, from a luncheon to a cocktail party. There is simply no end to the variety of chicken dishes which one can create. In fact, despite the concentrated time during which we tested recipes for this book, we never tired of chicken; we laughed when one caught the other ordering chicken in a restaurant!

It is our hope that you celebrate your success with chicken; may your guests cheer each and every time you serve it, and may they never cry "Fowl !!"

before you cook

- Bone up on *chickinformation* (page 177)! Of particular interest are tips for low cholesterol cooking and hints about equipment.
- Turn to *nest eggs* (page 171) and don't miss the *freezer labels*!
- Please note that parentheses in the menus indicate those dishes for which no recipes are included.

TABLE OF CONTENTS

1

company chicks

COQ au VIN

RICE PILAF (page 89)

ORANGE MAPLE CARROTS

GRAPEFRUIT and AVOCADO SALAD

Serves 4

COQ au VIN

1 Season:

8 serving pieces frying chicken

with:

Salt

Freshly ground pepper

Broil, turning to brown on all sides. Set aside.

2 In flameproof au gratin dish, sauté:

½ cup chopped carrots

1 clove minced garlic

2 shallots, minced

¼ cup chopped fresh celery leaves

2 tablespoons chopped fresh parsley
(2 teaspoons dried; added at Step 3)

in:

2 tablespoons butter

2 ounces salt pork, minced

Drain off excess fat.

3 Add:

1 teaspoon marjoram

½ teaspoon thyme

1 teaspoon salt

¼ teaspoon freshly ground pepper

1 teaspoon Worcestershire sauce

2 tablespoons chili sauce

Mix carefully to blend.

4 Add:

1 bay leaf

2 cups dry white wine

Bring to a boil and simmer for 5 minutes.

5 Place browned chicken in pan with wine and vegetables. Add:

¾ cup frozen tiny onions

Simmer for 50 minutes.

6 Remove bay leaf and add:

¾ pound mushrooms, sliced

Simmer 10 minutes longer.

7 Season to taste. If necessary, thicken sauce with:

Instant blend flour

Serve chicken on a hot platter topped with sauce and vegetables. Can be cooked ahead and reheated.

Coq au Vin

ORANGE MAPLE CARROTS

1 Cook over medium heat until carrots are tender:
> **5 cups sliced carrots**
> **2 tablespoons butter**
> **2 tablespoons maple syrup**
> **3 tablespoons frozen orange juice concentrate**
> **1 cup water**

Add extra water if necessary to prevent sticking and burning.

2 When carrots are tender, stir in:
> **¼ teaspoon salt**
> **¼ teaspoon freshly ground pepper**
> **Few grinds fresh nutmeg**

Cook over medium heat, stirring often, until 2-3 tablespoons liquid remains.

3 Thicken with:
> **Instant blend flour**

4 Stir in:
> **3 tablespoons orange marmalade**

5 Sprinkle with:
> **Chopped fresh parsley**

Can be made ahead and reheated in double boiler, oven, or microwave.

GRAPEFRUIT and AVOCADO SALAD

1 On individual salad plates, prepare beds of:
> **Bibb lettuce, broken into bite-sized pieces**

2 Arrange over lettuce:
> **Pink and white grapefruit sections**
> **Avocado, sliced and sprinkled with lemon juice**

(To section grapefruit, peel with knife. Then slice between membranes to remove sections.)

3 Top with:
> **Raspberry Vinegar Dressing (page 163)**
> or:
> **Chutney Dressing (page 163)**

The Chutney Dressing complements curry dishes nicely.

To prepare in advance: (1)Section grapefruit and refrigerate. Drain well before assembling salads. (2)The avocado can be peeled, sliced, and sprinkled with lemon juice. Refrigerate in airtight container. (3)Wash, dry, and break lettuce. Store in plastic bag.

CHICKEN DUGLÉRÉ
MUSHROOMS STUFFED with PEAS
PARSLEY BUTTER
NEW POTATOES (page 70)
TIC TAC TOE SALAD
Serves 4

CHICKEN DUGLÉRÉ

1 In flameproof au gratin dish, sauté:
>**½ pound of mushrooms, sliced**

in:
>**1 tablespoon butter**

Remove mushrooms with slotted spoon; set aside.

2 Add to mushroom juice in skillet:
>**⅔ cup dry white wine**
>**½ cup water**
>**1 stalk celery with leaves**
>**1 scallion, sliced**
>**2 tablespoons fresh chopped parsley (2 teaspoons dried)**
>**1 bay leaf**
>**8 peppercorns**

Simmer for 15 minutes. Strain; return strained liquid to pan.

3 Poach for 5 minutes on each side in strained liquid:
>**4 chicken breasts, boned, skinned and halved***

Remove with slotted spoon and set aside.

4 Measure poaching liquid and add enough:
>**Chicken broth***

to make 1⅓ cups. Return to skillet.

5 Add and bring to a boil:
>**2 tablespoons tomato paste**
>**1 teaspoon sugar**
>**4 teaspoons grated Parmesan cheese**

6 Thicken with:
>**Instant blend flour**

7 Fold in:
>**½ cup heavy cream, whipped***

Return chicken to sauce. Add sautéed mushrooms and spoon sauce over all. Cover pan and reheat just until boiling point.

* If you wish to use part dark meat, poach the dark meat for 5 minutes on each side before adding white meat. Then poach white and dark meat 5 more minutes on each side, totalling 20 minutes for dark meat and 10 minutes for white.

** For a lower calorie version, use ⅓ cup milk in place of whipped cream. This should be added at Step 4 with the chicken broth.

To prepare in advance, follow recipe through Step 6 and refrigerate until serving time.

MUSHROOMS STUFFED with PEAS

1 Mix and allow to stand 30 minutes:
   ¼ cup melted butter
   1 clove garlic, cut in half

2 Preheat oven to 375°.

3 Wash, drain and remove stems from
   20 large mushrooms
   Brush mushrooms, inside and out, with garlic butter.

4 Sauté in remaining butter:
   2 tablespoons minced shallots

5 Cook according to package directions:
   1 10-ounce package frozen peas
   Drain.

6 Purée peas and season with:
   ½ teaspoon salt
   ¼ teaspoon freshly ground pepper
   ⅛ teaspoon freshly grated nutmeg
   Stir in sautéed shallots.

7 Fill mushroom caps with puréed pea mixture. Sprinkle with:
   Freshly grated Parmesan cheese
   Place in flameproof serving dish.

8 Bake in preheated oven for 15 minutes.

This may be prepared through Step 6, covered with plastic wrap and refrigerated until cooking time. Bring to room temperature before baking.

Lovely as either an hors d'oeuvre or as a vegetable side dish.

Adapted from BEGINNING AGAIN, More Hors d'Oeuvres — Rockdale Ridge Press.

18

TIC TAC TOE SALAD *Individual Servings*

1 Cut into ½" strips and place on salad plate:
   ½ cup romaine

2 Lay on top of lettuce:
   3-4" square well-drained pimiento
   If desired drizzle with anchovy oil.

3 On top of the pimiento, make a tic-tac-toe grid out of:
   4 strips (4" × ½") well-drained hearts of palm

4 Place in the grid any of the following:
   Cherry tomatoes
   Anchovies
   Marinated artichokes
   Olives

5 Serve with:
   Vinaigrette Dressing (page 164)

This salad can be assembled ahead if all ingredients are well-drained.

Chick-Tac-Toe

CHICKEN KIEV á la RUSSE
or
CHICKEN KIEV
EGGPLANT PROVENÇAL
CELERY ROOT and APPLE SALAD
Serves 8

CHICKEN KIEV á la RUSSE

1 Blend together:
   1 stick sweet butter, softened
   ½ teaspoon dill weed
   2 teaspoons chopped fresh parsley
   2 teaspoons chopped fresh chives
Gently stir in:
   3 tablespoons black caviar, drained

2 Shape butter into 8 sticks (2½"x½"x½"); freeze.

3 Chill in plastic bag:
   4 1-pound chicken breasts; split, skinned, and boned
While chicken and butter are chilling, follow steps 2 and 3.

4 Place in shallow dish:
   ⅓ cup Italian Bread Crumbs (page 176)
Set aside.

5 Place on a plate:
   ⅓ cup flour
Set aside.

6 Pound chilled chicken breasts one at a time, in the plastic bag to ³/₁₆" thickness using flat side of a meat tenderizing mallet.

7 Sprinkle with:
   Salt
   White pepper

8 Lay a stick of chilled butter in the middle of each chicken breast. Cover butter with filet. (The filet is the thin, loose strip of meat attached to the breast.) Brush seams with:
   1 slightly beaten egg

9 Fold 1 long side of chicken over butter. Press seams together and brush with egg.

10 Fold 2 short sides of chicken over butter. Brush seams together with egg.

20

11 Place in refrigerator on pan lined with waxed paper, seam side down, until all are rolled.

12 Add to remaining egg (beating only slightly to avoid forming bubbles):
   2 teaspoons milk

13 Dip rolled chicken in flour, covering completely but lightly. Pat excess off.

14 Dip in egg mixture. Use pastry brush to cover *completely.* Let excess drip off.

15 Place in crumb mixture. Cover evenly and completely. Remember to cover edges as well; breading the edges creates a seal that keeps the butter from running out.

16 Place on wire rack and chill 2 hours or more.

17 Preheat oven to 400°.

18 Bake in lightly greased dish in preheated oven for 15 minutes, turning once.

19 Remove from oven and serve at once.

For traditional **CHICKEN KIEV,** omit the caviar.

chickchat
A simple step-by-step method unravels this culinary mystery.

21

EGGPLANT PROVENÇAL

1 Prepare according to package directions, until al dente:
   3 ounces spinach noodles
   Drain; place in flameproof au gratin dish.

2 Prepare according to package directions:
   1 10-ounce package frozen French style string beans
   Drain; season to taste. Place over noodles.

3 Preheat broiler.

4 Peel and slice into ¾" slices:
   1 medium eggplant

5 Brush both sides with:
   4 tablespoons olive oil

6 Sprinkle with:
   Salt
   Freshly ground pepper
   Place on baking sheet. Brown 6" from broiler 4-6 minutes on each side, or until lightly browned. Arrange on noodles.

7 Sprinkle with:
   2 tablespoons grated Parmesan cheese
   ¼ cup bread crumbs

8 Sauté until transparent:
   ⅔ cup frozen chopped onion (½ cup fresh)
   in:
   1 tablespoon olive oil

9 Add and continue cooking for 5 minutes:
   ½ pound mushrooms, sliced

10 Mix onions and mushrooms with:
   2 15-ounce cans tomato sauce
   2 teaspoons chopped fresh basil (½ teaspoon dried)
   2 teaspoons chopped fresh oregano (½ teaspoon dried)
   ½ teaspoon chopped fresh thyme (⅛ teaspoon dried)
   3 tablespoons chopped fresh parsley (2 teaspoons dried)
   ½ teaspoon freshly ground pepper
   Pour over eggplant.

11 Preheat oven to 325°.

12 Bake for 50 minutes, or until heated through and bubbling. Top with:
   4 ounces provolone cheese, shredded
   Bake 10 minutes more, until cheese melts.

This is a wonderful dish to make in summer to take advantage of the pungent flavors of fresh herbs.

Buy a good quality provolone cheese to insure a smooth texture. Lower quality cheeses tend to become stringy.

To prepare in advance, follow recipe through Step 10.

CELERY ROOT and APPLE SALAD

1 Peel and slice:
> **2½ cups celery root (celeriac)**

Cover with boiling water and cook 20 minutes. Drain and dry on paper towels. Cool to room temperature.

2 Peel and slice:
> **4-6 apples to make 4 cups (Granny Smith, Winesap, Jonathan, or McIntosh)**

Sprinkle with:
> **1 tablespoon fresh lemon juice**

3 Blend with wire whisk:
> **1½ teaspoons dill weed**
> **1½ teaspoons fresh chopped parsley (1 teaspoon dried)**
> **¾ teaspoon salt**
> **⅛ teaspoon freshly ground pepper**
> **¾ cup mayonnaise**
> **6 tablespoons sour cream**

4 Stir in celeriac and apple; chill.

5 Sprinkle with:
> **⅓ cup chopped walnuts**
> **Freshly ground pepper to taste**

Waldorf salad with a twist!

Egg Plant

CHICKEN OSCAR

1 Chill in plastic bag:
   4 small chicken breasts (¾-pound); split, skinned, and boned

2 Place on a plate:
   ⅓ cup Italian Bread Crumbs (page 176)
   Set aside.

3 Place on a plate:
   ⅓ cup flour
   Set aside.

4 In a shallow dish, beat slightly with a fork without forming bubbles:
   1 egg
   2 teaspoons milk
   Set aside.

5 Pound chilled chicken breasts, one at a time, in the plastic bag to ¼" thickness, using flat side of a meat tenderizing mallet.

6 Sprinkle with:
   Salt
   White pepper

7 If chicken is moist, pat dry. Dip in flour, covering completely but lightly. Pat excess off.

8 Dip in egg mixture. Use pastry brush to cover *completely*. Let excess drip off.

9 Place in crumb mixture. Cover evenly and completely. Remember to cover edges as well.

10 Refrigerate on wire rack for 2 hours.

11 Steam until tender (do not overcook):
   1½ pounds fresh asparagus
   Drain and season.

12 Have at room temperature, well drained:

    6½ ounces jumbo lump backfin crabmeat, canned or fresh

13 Prepare:

    1 measure Béarnaise Sauce (below)

14 Preheat oven to 500°.

15 Bake breaded chicken in lightly greased dish in preheated oven for 15 minutes, turning once.

16 Remove from oven; top individual servings with asparagus, crabmeat, and Béarnaise Sauce.

BÉARNAISE SAUCE   *Makes 1¼ cups*

1 Simmer to reduce one half:

    2 tablespoons dry white wine
    2 tablespoons Tarragon Vinegar (page 174)
    2 teaspoons minced shallots
    1 sprig fresh tarragon (¾ teaspoon dried)

2 Heat to boiling:

    1 stick butter

3 Place in food processor with steel blade, at room temperature, the wine vinegar mixture and:

    ½ cup egg yolks (about 6)
    ½ teaspoon salt
    ½ teaspoon freshly ground pepper

Blend with two ON/OFF pulses.

3 With food processor ON, add butter in a slow steady stream. This should take about 1 minute.

Keep warm over hot, not boiling, water until ready to serve. Or if you own an electric tray, place sauce in serving dish on warmed tray.

Extra sauce served at room temperature is a delicious way to disguise leftover chicken.

chickchat
An elegant favorite adapted for economical eating.

POTATO PUFFS

1 Bake:
>**4 large red potatoes**

When cool enough to handle, cut in half and scoop out potato, taking care not to tear skin.

2 Mash and add:
>**1½ cups grated sharp cheddar cheese (6 ounces)**
>**2 tablespoons minced onion**
>**1 2-ounce jar pimiento, minced**
>**2 eggs, beaten**
>**½ teaspoon salt**
>**¼ teaspoon freshly ground pepper**

3 Pack back into 4 of the potato skins. Sprinkle with:
>**Buttered bread crumbs**

4 Bake at 350° for 30 minutes or until heated through.

May be prepared ahead through Step 3.

GREEN BEAN and MUSHROOM SALAD

1 Place in plastic bag:
>**2 cups green beans, cooked and drained**
>**¼ cup Vinaigrette Dressing (page 164)**

Turn bag several times to coat beans with dressing; marinate several hours or overnight in refrigerator.

2 In large salad bowl, toss marinated beans with:
>**6 cups bibb lettuce, broken into pieces**
>**1 cup raw sliced mushrooms**
>**Vinaigrette to coat**

3 Garnish with:
>**Alfalfa sprouts**

CHICKEN BORDELAISE
WILD RICE with ASPARAGUS
CELERY CABBAGE SALAD
Serves 4

CHICKEN BORDELAISE

1 Place in plastic bag:
4 whole chicken legs, disjointed and skinned

2 Mix and pour over chicken, turning to coat.
¼ cup lemon juice
½ teaspoon salt
A few grinds of pepper
1 clove garlic, peeled and halved
2 tablespoons oil
Marinate chicken for 2 hours at room temperature or overnight in the refrigerator.

3 Place in 3-quart flameproof casserole:
1½ pounds mushrooms, sliced
3 cups peeled tomato wedges, seeds removed
2 cups white Bordeaux wine
2 tablespoons chopped fresh parsley (2 teaspoons dried)
1 cup sweet red peppers in julienne strips
Bring to a boil; reduce to medium heat and simmer 25 minutes.

4 While the sauce is simmering, remove chicken from marinade. Dry on paper towels. Discard garlic and reserve marinade.

5 Sear chicken on both sides in:
4 tablespoons butter
Remove from skillet and set aside.

6 Add to skillet:
3 cups Vidalia or Bermuda onions, thinly sliced
Sauté over medium heat for 15 minutes pulling onion rings apart. Return chicken to skillet and continue cooking, turning frequently. After 15 minutes, remove onions and add to sauce. Pour reserved marinade into skillet, cover, and continue cooking chicken for 20 minutes. Place chicken and liquid in casserole with sauce.

➡

7 Thicken slightly with:
   Instant blend flour

May be prepared ahead through Step 3.

WILD RICE with ASPARAGUS

1 Rinse well in a fine strainer:
   4 ounces (¾ cup) wild rice

2 In a 2-quart saucepan, bring to a boil:
   ½ teaspoon salt
   2½ cups boiling water
   Mix rice in and return to a boil. Cover and reduce heat,
   simmering until tender (40-50 minutes). Drain off any
   excess liquid.

3 Trim; then boil or steam until tender:
   1 pound fresh asparagus
   Drain.

4 Melt together and set aside:
   2 tablespoons butter
   ½ teaspoon freshly ground pepper
   ½ teaspoon salt

5 Preheat oven to 325°.

6 Sauté 3-4 minutes over medium-high heat:
   ½ pound mushrooms, thinly sliced
   3 tablespoons chopped shallots
   in:
   1 tablespoon butter
   Set mushrooms and shallots aside.

7 In same skillet sauté 3-4 minutes over medium-high heat:
   1½ cups diced celery
   adding to skillet:
   1 tablespoon butter
   Mix celery with rice.

28

9 In a 6″ x 9″ flameproof serving dish, layer vegetables as follows: spread half of the rice and celery in the dish; cover with half of the mushroom mixture; lay half the asparagus over this, and top with half the reserved butter. Repeat with remaining ingredients.

10 Top with:
   ¼ cup pine nuts
   Warm in preheated oven for 30 minutes or until heated through; cover with foil for the first 15 minutes of baking.

This recipe can be prepared ahead and reheated at serving time.

CELERY CABBAGE SALAD

1 Wash, thoroughly drain, and thinly slice:
   1 celery cabbage to make 4 cups
2 Place cabbage in a salad bowl and toss with:
   ½ teaspoon salt
   ½ teaspoon freshly ground pepper
   1 teaspoon celery seed
   ¼-⅓ cup Red Wine Vinegar and Oil Dressing (page 162)
   4 tablespoons corn relish (optional)

Try this with napa instead of celery cabbage.

29

POULET CHAMPAGNE aux CHAMPIGNONS

1 Sprinkle:
    ½ cup diced avocado
with:
    2 teaspoons lime juice

2 Sauté, stirring frequently to prevent burning:
    ½ cup chopped macadamia nuts
in:
    1 tablespoon butter
Remove with slotted spoon and set aside.

3 Sauté for 8 minutes until mushrooms give up their juices:
    ½ pound mushrooms, sliced
    1 tablespoon chopped shallots
in:
    1 tablespoon butter

4 Add and continue sautéeing for 2 minutes:
    ½ cup diced artichoke bottoms
Remove vegetables with slotted spoon and set aside.

5 Add to skillet:
    1 tablespoon butter
    1 tablespoon oil

6 Sauté in butter and oil, turning to sear on all sides:
    8 fryer thighs and breasts, skinned and boned
Place chicken in a flameproof dish.

7 Drain sautéed vegetables, reserving juice. Add to juice:
    1 teaspoon chicken base
    1 teaspoon frozen orange juice concentrate
    1 cup champagne
Pour over chicken and simmer 10 minutes, or until chicken is tender, turning and basting occasionally.

8 Thicken pan juices with:
   Instant blend flour
9 Combine sautéed vegetables with:
   ¼ cup sour cream
   Stir into chicken gravy. Heat just to boiling point.
10 Sprinkle with avocado and macadamia nuts.

May be prepared in advance through Step 5. Refrigerate and complete at serving time.

The Family Way
Substitute dry white wine or chicken broth for champagne.

chickchat

A delicious way to use up that leftover bottle of champagne — and there will still be enough to whip up some Champagne Salad Dressing (page 163).

Poulet de Paris

TOMATO FLORENTINE

Homegrown tomatoes make this especially delicious.

1 Preheat oven to 375°.

2 Scoop seeds and juice from:
4 medium tomatoes

3 Sprinkle inside lightly with:
Salt
Freshly ground pepper

4 Fill with:
1 measure Creamed Spinach (page 81)

5 Top with:
4 teaspoons grated Romano cheese
Bake in preheated oven 20 minutes in a flameproof serving dish.

If you wish to get a head start on this recipe, prepare tomatoes (Step 2 only) and Creamed Spinach. Drain tomatoes and complete Steps 3-5 one hour before baking.

TOSSED ASPARAGUS SALAD

1 Place in plastic bag:
1½ cups raw asparagus, cut into 1" pieces
Marinate several hours or overnight in refrigerator in:
2 tablespoons Red Wine Vinegar and Oil Dressing (page 162)

2 Toss marinated asparagus with:
4 cups head lettuce, broken into bite-sized pieces
⅓ cup sliced stuffed green olives
2 tablespoons corn relish
Additional dressing to coat

3 Garnish with:
12 cherry tomatoes
¼ cup pumpkin seeds

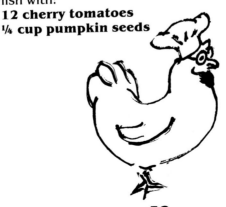

ROAST CAPON with PEACH STUFFING
(GREEN BEANS with SLIVERED ALMONDS)
GREEK SALAD
Serves 6

ROAST CAPON with PEACH STUFFING

1 Preheat oven to 275°.

2 Cut into ¾ " squares and spread out on a cookie sheet:
    5 ounces (3 cups) white bread
Dry in preheated oven for 15 minutes. Remove and set aside.

3 Change oven setting to 500°.

4 Remove all visible fat from:
    1 6-8 pound capon

5 Sauté 2 large chunks of fat in a large skillet over medium heat
until fat separates from tissue. Remove remaining chunk.
Brush capon with melted fat.

6 Add to skillet:
    1 cup frozen chopped onions (¾ cup fresh)
Sauté for 5 minutes.

7 Add to skillet:
    1½ cups diced celery
    ½ cup chopped celery leaves
Sauté 10 minutes more. Set aside.

8 Peel and dice:
    1 pound fresh peaches to make 2 cups
Set aside.

9 Blend well:
    1½ teaspoons chicken base
    1 beaten egg
    ⅛ teaspoon freshly ground pepper
    ½ teaspoon poultry seasoning
    **1 tablespoon chopped fresh parsley (1 teaspoon
       dried)**
    2 tablespoons water
Stir in:
    6 tablespoons additional water

→

10 Place dried bread in a large mixing bowl. Pour liquid ingredients, celery, and onions over bread and mix. Stir peaches in gently.

11 Sprinkle body and neck cavities of capon with:
Seasoned Salt (page 172)
Fill loosely with stuffing. Fasten neck skin to back with skewers; tuck legs and tail.

12 If there is extra stuffing, bake for 1¾ hours in a covered casserole with some chicken wings and necks on top to add flavor. Uncover for the last 15 minutes.

13 Place capon, breast side down, in greased roasting pan.

14 Place in preheated oven. After 10 minutes, turn capon over and reduce heat to 325°. Continue baking uncovered for 45 minutes.

15 Cover with foil and bake an additional 25 minutes per pound.

16 Let stand for 15 minutes before carving.

Superchicken (Cape On)

The superb flavor of capon, its larger portions of breast and thigh, and its size—6-9 pounds—make it perfect for company meals.

To produce capons, roosters are surgically desexed at age three weeks. They are then fed more grain proportionate to the weight they gain and are grown over a longer period of time than ordinary chickens. The result: DELICIOUS!

GREEK SALAD

1 Arrange in salad bowl:
> **9 cups romaine, bibb, or Boston lettuce, broken into bite-sized pieces**

2 Sprinkle with:
> **⅓ cup pine nuts**
> **1½ cups green seedless grapes**
> **⅓ cup crumbled Feta cheese, well drained**

3 When ready to serve, toss with
> **Dijon Dressing (page 162)**
> **Salt**
> **Freshly ground pepper**

The Company Way
Add an elegant touch by using walnut oil and raspberry vinegar to make the dressing.

Olympchix

CHICKEN PICCATA
HEARTS of PALM with PEPPERCORN HOLLANDAISE
SPINACH SALAD
Serves 4

CHICKEN PICCATA

1 Pound to ¼" thickness between two pieces of aluminum foil:
   4 ¾-pound chicken breasts; skinned, boned and halved

2 Sprinkle with:
   Salt
   Freshly ground pepper
   Flour

3 Sauté chicken in single layer for 1 minute in:
   1 tablespoon butter
   1 tablespoon olive oil
   Turn and cook on second side. Remove to platter and continue until all chicken is sautéed.

4 In same skillet, sauté:
   1 pound mushrooms, sliced
   adding to skillet:
   1 tablespoon butter
   1 tablespoon olive oil
   Remove with slotted spoon, reserving juices; set aside.

5 Add to mushroom juice in skillet:
   ½ cup dry white wine
   ¼ cup freshly squeezed lemon juice
   Deglaze* pan and simmer to reduce liquid to 1 cup.

6 Add:
   3 tablespoons capers, drained
   2 teaspoons grated Parmesan cheese

7 Return chicken and mushrooms to skillet and simmer for 3 minutes; turn and simmer 2 minutes more.

8 If necessary, thicken pan juices with:
   Instant blend flour

9 Sprinkle with:
   ¼ cup chopped fresh parsley

10 Garnish with:
   Thin lemon slices

*To deglaze is to add liquid to cooking pan and simmer, scraping gently to loosen sediment. This forms the base for a sauce.

chickchat

Traditionally made with veal, Chicken Piccata is Elegant, Economical and Easy!

HEARTS OF PALM with PEPPERCORN HOLLANDAISE

1 Preheat oven to 325°.

2 Wash, drain and dry:
   1 7-ounce can Hearts of Palm
   Split lengthwise into equal pieces.

3 Place in covered flameproof serving dish. Bake in preheated oven for 10-15 minutes or until heated through. Serve with:
   Peppercorn Hollandaise (below)

PEPPERCORN HOLLANDAISE SAUCE

Makes ¾ cup

1 Heat to boiling:
   1 stick butter

2 Crush to smooth paste with meat tenderizer mallet or kitchen mallet:
   1 teaspoon peppercorns packed in wine vinegar, well drained
   ¼ teaspoon salt

3 Place crushed peppercorns in food processor with the following at room temperature:
   3 egg yolks (¼ cup)
   3 tablespoons fresh lemon juice
   Using steel knife, blend with ON/OFF pulses.

4 With food processor ON, add butter in a slow steady stream. (This should take about 1 minute.)

Keep warm over hot, not boiling, water until ready to serve. Or if you own an electric tray, place sauce on warmed tray.

37

SPINACH SALAD

1 Mix and refrigerate 1-2 hours:
   ½ cup Dijon Dressing (page 162)
   1 tablespoon sugar
   ¼ cup chopped shallots
   ¼ teaspoon paprika
   ¼ teaspoon celery salt

2 Wash, dry, trim, and tear into bite-sized pieces:
   1 pound fresh spinach

3 Fry, drain, and crumble:
   ¼ pound bacon

4 Toss spinach with half the bacon and:
   ¾ cup fresh mushrooms, sliced
   Half of an 11-ounce can Mandarin oranges, drained

5 When ready to serve, add:
   1 medium, ripe avocado, sliced
   Toss with sufficient dressing to coat.

6 Top with remaining bacon and oranges, and sprinkle generously with:
   Freshly ground pepper

BUFFALO CHICKEN WINGS
DILLY VEGETABLES
ONION QUICHE
MUSHROOMS PROVOLONE
OLD FASHIONED CHOPPED LIVER
Serves 8

BUFFALO CHICKEN WINGS

1 Preheat oven to 400°.

2 Prepare:
3 pounds chicken wings
by cutting wings at joints to make three pieces; discard tips.

3 Sprinkle very lightly with:
Garlic salt
Bake in preheated oven in foil-lined pan for 20 minutes, turning after 10 minutes.

4 To crisp, broil 3-5 minutes on each side after baking. Drain on paper towels.

5 Mix in saucepan and heat to boiling:
¼ cup butter
6 ounces tomato juice
½ cup cayenne pepper sauce
½ teaspoon freshly ground pepper
Cayenne pepper*

6 Pour ¼ cup hot sauce into a large plastic lidded bowl. Place chicken wings in bowl, cover, and shake gently to coat wings with sauce.

7 Serve in a basket or on a platter with dishes of:
Blue Cheese Dressing (page 166)
Celery sticks
Remaining hot sauce

*Use cayenne pepper as follows:
½ teaspoon for Mild Wings
1 teaspoon for Hot Wings
1½ teaspoons for Dare Devil Wings

The Company Way
Use only the drumettes **(Cutting Wings into Drumettes, page 192)**

39

DILLY VEGETABLES

1 Mix in plastic bag:

1 16-ounce can Blue Lake string beans, drained
½ cup thinly sliced leeks

plus 1 cup each of any 6 of the following:

Sliced cucumber
Sliced yellow squash
Sliced celery
Sliced carrots
Sliced mushrooms
Cauliflower buds
Broccoli buds and / or sliced stems
Asparagus tips
Sliced white radishes
Sliced kohlrabi
Sliced Jerusalem artichokes
Sliced zucchini

2 Pour over vegetables:

Italian Dressing (page 162) to coat

Refrigerate overnight, turning bag occasionally to distribute dressing.

3 A few hours before serving, drain very thoroughly and add:

1 cup cherry tomatoes
1 cup drained, sliced black olives,
1 13½-ounce can pimiento, cut into 1" squares

4 Mix with wire whisk and blend with vegetables:

¼ cup sour cream
½ cup mayonnaise
2 tablespoons chili sauce
1 tablespoon fresh lemon juice
½ teaspoon grated lemon rind
1 tablespoon dill weed
½ teaspoon salt
¼ teaspoon freshly ground pepper

A salad spinner is super for draining vegetables.

Red radishes are a colorful addition to the assortment of vegetables. Because the color tends to run, marinate them separately and add at Step 3.

ONION QUICHE

Makes 12 slices

1 Preheat broiler.

2 Line 9″ pie plate or quiche pan with:
>   **Unbaked pie crust**

3 Place 2″ from preheated broiler and broil for 1-2 minutes or until lightly browned. Watch carefully to prevent burning. Cool on wire rack.

4 Change oven setting to 375°.

5 Fry until crisp:
>   **6 slices bacon, cut into thin strips**

Remove from fat with slotted spoon and drain on paper towels.

6 Add to bacon fat and cook until transparent:
>   **2 cups chopped Vidalia or sweet onions**

Drain off fat.

7 Beat together:
>   **2 eggs plus 1 egg yolk**
>   **¾ cup sour cream**
>   **½ teaspoon salt**
>   **¼ teaspoon freshly ground pepper**
>   **1 tablespoon snipped chives (1 teaspoon dried)**

8 Add onion and bacon to egg mixture; blend and pour into prepared pie shell. Sprinkle with:
>   **½ teaspoon caraway seed**
>   **2 teaspoons grated Parmesan cheese**

9 Bake in preheated oven for 18 minutes. Cool on wire rack for 5 minutes before slicing.

Fowl Ball

MUSHROOMS PROVOLONE

1 Preheat oven to 450°.

2 Remove stems from:
   2 pounds mushrooms

3 Sauté until limp:
   ¼ cup minced scallions
   2 cloves minced garlic
   in:
   2 tablespoons butter

4 Add:
   1½ cups dry white wine
   Simmer 5 minutes.

5 Place mushroom caps in a flameproof serving dish with wine mixture and:
   ¼ cup butter

6 Bake in preheated oven for 12 minutes on bottom shelf of oven.

7 Pour off juice; simmer to reduce to ½ cup.

8 Thicken with:
   Instant blend flour
   Pour back over mushrooms.

9 Return to oven until piping hot, about 7 minutes.

10 Spread over mushrooms:
   2 cups shredded provolone cheese
   Return to oven until cheese is melted, about 3 minutes.

This recipe may be prepared in advance through Step 8; refrigerate and finish when ready to serve.

Adapted from "Mushrooms Mozzarella" — Beginning Again, More Hors d'Oeuvres by Rockdale Ridge Press, 1981.

chickchat
Have a cocktail party for "chicken feed"!

OLD FASHIONED CHOPPED LIVER

Makes 1 cup

1 Wash and cut away membranes and green spots from:
    3 large (5 small) VERY FRESH chicken livers

2 Sauté liver with:
    ⅔ cup frozen chopped onion (½ cup fresh)
in:
    1 tablespoon Chicken Fat (page 173)
until liver is no longer pink.

3 Refrigerate until chilled through.

4 Coarsely chop:
    1 hard-boiled egg
Set aside.

5 Coarsely chop liver. The food processor is excellent for this; chop with steel knife using ON/OFF pulses.

6 Combine liver and eggs. Stir in:
    1-3 teaspoons softened Chicken Fat
    Salt and freshly ground pepper to taste
using enough fat to hold the mixture together.

7 Mold in a small bowl lined with plastic wrap.

8 Serve with:
    Party rye
    Rye crackers

CURRIED CHICKEN
SESAME RICE
ROMAINE DIJON with
PECORINO ROMANO
Serves 8

CURRIED CHICKEN

1 Sauté:

> **1 pound fresh mushrooms, sliced**

in:

> **2 tablespoons butter**

Remove with slotted spoon, leaving juice in skillet. Set mushrooms aside.

2 Add to skillet:

> **2 tablespoons butter**

and sauté until limp:

> **1½ cups chopped sweet onions**
> **1 clove minced garlic**

3 Stir in:

> **1½ tablespoons instant blend flour**
> **1 teaspoon salt**
> **1 tablespoon curry powder***
> **½ teaspoon lemon pepper**
> **2 teaspoons sugar**
> **½ teaspoon Dijon mustard**

4 Add:

> **2 cups chicken broth**
> **½ cup half & half**
> **2 tablespoons chutney sauce**

5 Cook over low heat until thickened, stirring frequently.

6 Add:

> **2 tablespoons chopped candied ginger**
> **1 cup white raisins**
> **2 cups chopped Granny Smith apples**
> **1 cup fresh tomatoes; peeled, seeded, and coarsely chopped**
> **¼ cup shredded coconut (unsweetened)**

7 Cover and simmer for 20 minutes.

8 Stir in sautéed mushrooms and:
   3½ cups Cooked Chicken Breast (page 186)
   2 tablespoons lime juice

9 Serve with dishes of:
   Rice
   Chutney
   Chopped green onions
   Shredded coconut
   Chopped bacon
   Chopped peanuts

* For strong curry flavor, use 2 tablespoons curry powder.

This recipe may be made ahead and reheated in a casserole in the oven.

SESAME RICE

1 Have ready:
   8 cups cooked rice

2 Sauté:
   ⅔ cup sliced green onions
   ⅓ tablespoon toasted sesame seeds
   in:
   4 tablespoons butter
   Stir into hot rice.

3 Season to taste with:
   Salt
   Freshly ground pepper

Prepare in advance and reheat in oven in covered baking dish.

ROMAINE DIJON with PECORINO ROMANO

1 Toss:
   16 cups romaine, broken into bite-sized pieces
   with:
   1 pint cherry tomatoes
   Dijon Dressing (page 162) to coat

2 Top with:
   1½ cups shredded Pecorino Romano cheese

chickchat

Go to work today; have a party tonight. This Curried Chicken menu is a perfect do-ahead party supper.

your chickchat

chicken like grandma used to make

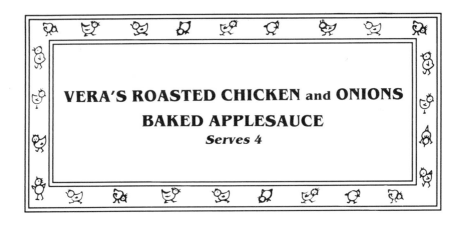

VERA'S ROASTED CHICKEN and ONIONS

BAKED APPLESAUCE

Serves 4

VERA'S ROASTED CHICKEN and ONIONS

1 Peel and slice:
   2-3 large Bermuda or Vidalia onions to make 4 cups

2 Peel and halve:
   Approximately 8 new red potatoes, 2″ diameter, to make 2 cups

3 Sauté onions and potatoes over medium heat for 15 minutes, in:
   2 tablespoons butter
   Turn frequently.

4 While onions and potatoes are cooking, cut into serving pieces:
   1 4-pound fryer.
   Place chicken in single layer in flameproof serving dish. Brown under broiler, turning legs and thighs to brown on all sides. Pour off fat.

5 Change oven setting to 500°

6 Remove chicken from dish. Lay sautéed onions and potatoes in dish and sprinkle with:
   ½ teaspoon Seasoned Salt (page 172)
   Place chicken pieces over vegetables, skin side up.

7 Mix:
   1½ cups dry white wine or water
   1½ teaspoons chicken base
   Pour over chicken and vegetables.

8 Place in preheated oven. Reduce heat immediately to 275°. Bake 2 hours, basting every 15 minutes and turning legs and thighs several times to brown on all sides.

Additional necks (skin removed), backs, and wings can be placed in dish under potatoes and onions for extra rich gravy. Remove before serving.

48

BAKED APPLESAUCE

1 Place in covered flameproof casserole:

> **6 cups Granny Smith apples, peeled, cored and finely chopped in food processor**
> **1 cinnamon stick**
> **½ cup sugar**
> **½ lemon, rind only (Frozen Lemon Peels, below)**

2 Bake at 325° for 40 minutes or until apples are tender. Remove cinnamon stick and lemon rind. Add more sugar as needed.

Prepare in quantity and freeze for future use.

Roasted Chicken

49

CHICKEN PAPRIKASH

1 Season:
> **8 serving pieces frying chicken**

with:
> **Salt**
> **Freshly ground pepper**

3 Brown under broiler, turning to brown all sides.

4 Using a deep, covered flameproof serving dish, sauté:
> **1 cup frozen chopped onions (¾ cup fresh)**

in:
> **2 tablespoons bacon fat, chicken fat or other fat**

5 Mix with onion:
> **1 small clove garlic, squeezed in garlic press**
> **2 tablespoons Hungarian paprika**
> **1 cup chicken stock**
> **⅛ teaspoon freshly ground pepper**
> **½ cup chopped green pepper**
> **3 tablespoons tomato paste**

6 Place chicken in dish; cover with sauce.

7 Bring to boil; cover and simmer 45 minutes, basting occasionally. Add water if necessary. A heat-diffusing pad under the dish will help prevent sticking.

8 Skim fat; cook uncovered 15 minutes to reduce sauce. Season to taste.

9 Thicken to desired consistency with:
> **Instant blend flour**

Equally as delicious if prepared ahead and reheated.

SPAETZLE

1 In 2-quart mixing bowl, beat:
> **3 large eggs**
> **¼ teaspoon nutmeg**
> **½ teaspoon salt**

2 Add and mix until blended:
> **3 cups flour**
> (The mixture will be stiff and lumpy)

3 Add gradually and beat until dough is smooth:
> **1 cup of milk**
> Cover with plastic wrap and let dough rest 15 minutes.

4 Place dough in spaetzle maker over saucepan containing:
> **2 quarts boiling water**
> **½ teaspoon salt**
> Scrape dough into water by turning handle of machine. (It is also possible, but more time consuming to press dough through a colander with spoon, ½ cup at a time.)

5 Cook in boiling water for 7 minutes, stirring occasionally to prevent sticking. (The spaetzle will float when done.)

6 Drain; rinse with cold water and drain again. Toss with:
> **¼ cup melted butter**
> **Salt and freshly ground pepper to taste**

7 Reheat when ready to serve in covered casserole in 325° oven. Top with:
> **1 cup dry bread crumbs**
> browned in:
> **¼ cup butter**

A half measure is sufficient for this menu. We suggest that you make a whole measure and freeze leftovers. Reheat in a covered dish in the oven. Add buttered bread crumbs just before serving.

chickchat

Dreaming of a cozy winter dinner of Chicken Paprikash and spaetzel, we lugged a spaetzel maker all the way home from Vienna — only to discover that it is a standard item in every cookware shop in the states!

COLESLAW

1 In a large pot, shred:
   3-pound head of cabbage

2 Sprinkle with:
   1 teaspoon salt

3 Cover with:
   Boiling water
   Let stand 5 minutes.

4 Drain well. Squeeze excess water from cabbage. Toss with fork to aerate.

5 Mix with cabbage:
   ⅓ cup chopped fresh parsley
   1 tablespoon finely diced onion

6 Blend well:
   1 teaspoon cracked pepper
   2 tablespoons sugar
   ½ cup salad oil
   ½ cup cider vinegar
   2 tablespoons mustard seed* (optional)

7 Toss cabbage with dressing. Season to taste. Refrigerate 4 hours or overnight before serving.

This is a very tart slaw. For a milder version, substitute rice vinegar for cider vinegar.

* *The mustard seed has an interesting crunchy texture. Soak in water overnight and drain before using.*

Store leftover slaw in refrigerator in covered container.

BARBECUED CHICKEN
(BUTTERED LIMA BEANS)
WILTED LETTUCE SALAD
Serves 4

BARBECUED CHICKEN

1 Season:
  8 serving pieces frying chicken
with:
  Salt
  Freshly ground pepper
Place in baking pan, skin side down.

2 Broil, 6" from heat, until lightly browned. Turn and broil until second side is browned.

3 Drain accumulated fat. Turn chicken pieces skin side down and brush generously with:
  Barbecue Sauce I, II or III (pages 54-55)
Pour ½ cup water into pan to prevent burning.

4 Return pan to oven and continue broiling for about 5 minutes or until the sauce just begins to brown. Turn chicken pieces; brush with additional sauce and return to oven until just lightly browned.

5 Turn chicken; brush with additional sauce. Change oven setting to bake, and set at 350°. Bake 15 minutes; turn; brush with additional sauce and bake 15 minutes longer.

6 Skim grease from sauce in pan and serve over chicken pieces.

If sauce on bottom of pan begins to brown, pour an additional ½ cup of water into pan.

BARBECUE SAUCE I
Makes 2 cups

1 Sauté in a deep skillet or saucepan:
>**⅓ cup frozen chopped onion (¼ cup fresh)**
>**½ cup chopped celery**

in:
>**1 tablespoon butter or oil**

2 Add and blend well:
>**½ teaspoon freshly ground pepper**
>**2 tablespoons brown sugar, firmly packed**
>**1 teaspoon prepared yellow mustard**
>**1 tablespoon Worcestershire sauce**
>**2 tablespoons red wine vinegar**
>>**or 1 tablespoon red wine vinegar plus**
>>**1 tablespoon Basil Vinegar (page 174)**
>**¼ cup lemon juice**

3 Stir in:
>**½ cup water**
>**1 cup catsup**

Simmer for 20 minutes over medium heat.

For the best flavor, mix ahead and refrigerate several hours or overnight, before reheating to serve. Or make a large quantity and freeze in 1-cup containers for future use.

BARBECUE SAUCE II
Makes 1¾ cups

1 Blend well:
>**1½ teaspoons chili powder**
>**½ teaspoon onion salt**
>**½ teaspoon celery salt**
>**1½ teaspoons dry mustard**
>**½ teaspoon freshly ground pepper**

2 Stir in:
>**½ cup (4 ounces) brown sugar**

3 Add:
>**1 6-ounce can tomato paste**
>**1 teaspoon Worcestershire sauce**
>**1½ teaspoons vinegar**

Mix well.

4 Finally, blend in:
>**½ cup catsup**
>**¾ cup water**

This sauce freezes well.

BARBECUE SAUCE III

Makes 2 cups

1 Combine and mix to blend:

    4 cups catsup
    2 cups vinegar
    1 cup honey
    4 teaspoons salt
    ½ cup dehydrated onions
    ½ cup prepared mustard
    2 teaspoons chili powder
    2 teaspoons Worcestershire sauce
    1 teaspoon freshly ground pepper

2 Store in refrigerator.

This sauce keeps indefinitely and is also good for barbecued ribs.

WILTED LETTUCE SALAD

1 Fry until fat is separated and meat is crisp:
    ¼ pound ham fat, chopped
Remove ham with slotted spoon. Set aside.

2 Add to hot fat and sauté until wilted:
    2 tablespoons thinly sliced scallions

3 Stir in:
    1 teaspoon sugar
    ¼ cup vinegar

4 Break into pieces:
    1 head lettuce
or:
    8 cups assorted greens (leaf, bibb, Boston, romaine)

5 Place greens in salad bowl and top with:
    ½ cup avocado, sliced

6 Pour hot dressing over greens. Toss; top with ham fat pieces.
Serve at once with loads of:
    Freshly ground pepper

Sliced hard-boiled eggs make an attractive garnish.

chickchat

As we arrived at our favorite Kentucky vegetable farm one morning, we caught the farmer smacking his lips as he gazed over a field of young lettuce plants. He grinned and explained to us that they were thinning the lettuce that day and his wife would cover the young lettuce leaves with her special hot ham dressing for dinner that night.

CHICKEN IN THE POT with
MATZO BALLS

MIX 'N' MATCH SALAD (page 161)
with **FRENCH DRESSING** (page 168)
Serves 4

CHICKEN IN THE POT

1 Place in steamer and steam for 30 minutes:
   8 pieces frying chicken (2 legs, 2 thighs, 2 breasts, halved)

2 Add after the first 15 minutes:
   3 cups carrots, cut into 3" pieces and split
   1 cup celery, cut into bite-sized pieces
   ⅔ cup frozen baby onions

3 Continue steaming for 15 minutes more or until carrots are tender.

4 Bring to a boil:
   3 cups Chicken Broth (page 173)*
   Matzo Balls (below)
   Remove from heat.

5 Place chicken and vegetables in a deep casserole with Matzo Balls; arrange attractively with carrots on top.

6 Pour broth over all.

7 Sprinkle with:
   1 tablespoon chopped fresh parsley

* The 3 cups may include the broth from the steamer. You may wish to thicken it slightly with:
   Instant blend flour

Serve in flat soup plates.

chickchat
Chicken-in-the-Pot is a delicious homestyle meal often served in New York delis.

MATZO BALLS

Makes 8-10

1 Beat with fork:
> **3 tablespoons Chicken Fat (page 173) at room temperature**
> **2 large eggs**
> **1½ teaspoons chopped fresh parsley (½ teaspoon dried)**
> **1 teaspoon salt**

2 Stir in:
> **⅓ cup matzo cake meal**

3 Chill in refrigerator, covered, for 1 hour or more.

4 Roll into 1½'' balls.

5 Drop into:
> **2 quarts boiling water**
> If matzo balls stick to bottom of pot, loosen with spatula or pancake turner.

6 Cover pot and boil slowly for 30 minutes.

7 Remove with slotted spoon and drain.

May be prepared in advance and frozen. Thaw before rewarming. Although plain matzo meal is traditionally used, matzo cake meal makes a much lighter product.

Adapted from *IN THE BEGINNING, A Collection of Hors d'Oeuvres,* Rockdale Ridge Press.

ARROZ con POLLO
SPANISH VEGETABLES VINAIGRETTE
Serves 4

ARROZ con POLLO
(Spanish Chicken and Rice)

1 Season:
> **4 pound fryer, cut up**

with:
> **Salt**
> **Freshly ground pepper**
> **Paprika**

Brown under broiler on all sides.

2 Change oven setting to 350°.

3 In 3-quart flameproof casserole, sauté:
> **2 ounces chorizo sausage, crumbled**
> **or 2 ounces hot or mild Italian sausage, crumbled**

with;
> **⅓ cup frozen chopped onion (¼ cup fresh)**

(Choose a casserole with a tightly fitting lid for use in Step 6.)

4 When onions are wilted, add and continue sautéing 1-2 minutes:
> **1 cup raw rice**
> **1 clove minced garlic**

5 Add to casserole:
> **4 cups canned, strained crushed tomatoes**
> **2 teaspoons salt**
> **½ teaspoon freshly ground pepper**
> **½ teaspoon paprika**
> **¼ teaspoon powdered saffron**
> **1 bay leaf**
> **½ teaspoon oregano**
> **2 teaspoons chicken base**

Blend all ingredients well and bring to a boil.

6 Add chicken pieces and cover with sauce. Cover casserole tightly.

7 Bake in preheated oven for 30 minutes.

8 Stir in:
   1 10-ounce package frozen peas, thawed
   Continue baking 30 minutes more.

This dish is traditionally prepared with chorizo sausage. You may substitute either mild or hot Italian sausage to suit your palate.

The Company way
Add at Step 8:
   1 can artichoke hearts, rinsed and drained

chickchat

We first ate Arroz con Pollo while on a day trip outside of Havana. We had gotten a very early start, and by noon, when the tour stopped at a little roadside café, we were very hungry. The memory of that chicken and rice in our empty stomachs and the aura of warmth it created so far from home has stayed with us for over 30 years.

SPANISH VEGETABLES VINAIGRETTE

1 Drain well and place in container with lid:
   1 10-ounce can salad artichokes or artichoke hearts, halved, rinsed and drained on paper towels
   8 ounces mushrooms, sliced or whole, canned or fresh
   2 cups sliced celery
   1 10-ounce can hearts of palm, cut into ½" slices

2 Pour over vegetables:
   Vinaigrette Dressing II to coat (about 1 cup)
   (page 164)
   Toss gently. Refrigerate, covered, until time to serve.

This is plenty for eight people. Enjoy "planned-overs" for up to three days.

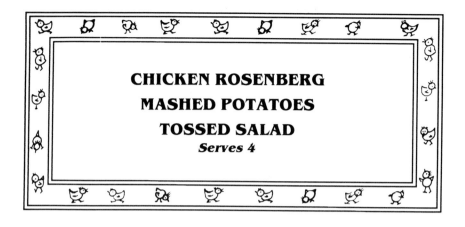

CHICKEN ROSENBERG
MASHED POTATOES
TOSSED SALAD
Serves 4

CHICKEN ROSENBERG

1 Preheat broiler.

2 Brown on all sides under broiler:
    1 4-pound fryer, cut up
Place in flameproof serving dish large enough to hold chicken in a single layer.

3 Change oven setting to 325°.

4 Finely chop in food processor with steel knife:
    2 medium carrots
    1 large stalk celery with leaves

5 Add:
    1 small onion
    Half of a 28-ounce can pear tomatoes in tomato
        purée*
    2 tablespoons sugar
    1 tablespoon instant blend flour
    1 teaspoon salt
    ½ teaspoon freshly ground pepper
    ½ teaspoon garlic salt
    2 tablespoons chopped fresh parsley (2 teaspoons
        dried)
    1 teaspoon Kitchen Bouquet
Process until tomatoes are finely chopped.
Pour into large mixing bowl. Process remaining half can of tomatoes and blend with sauce already in bowl.

6 Pour tomato sauce over chicken pieces.
Bake in preheated oven, uncovered, for 1½ hours, basting every 20 minutes with sauce. Turn once.

7 Skim off fat.

8 If necessary, thicken sauce with:
    Instant blend flour

*Divide tomatoes in half to avoid overflowing food processor.

Flavor is enhanced by preparing in advance and reheating before serving. This recipe also freezes well.

MASHED POTATOES

1 Cover with water and bring to a boil:
2 pounds red potatoes, peeled and quartered
Boil until tender.

2 Drain potatoes and place back on hot burner for 1-2 minutes to evaporate any remaining water.

3 Mash with potato masher. Add and continue to mash:
4 tablespoons butter
⅓ cup sour cream
1 teaspoon salt
Freshly ground pepper to taste

4 Add, ¼ cup at a time, as needed:
1-1½ cups milk, scalded

5 Beat until fluffy.

Cover and keep warm in double boiler or in 275° oven.

chickchat
Have your children ever tasted *real* mashed potatoes?

TOSSED SALAD

1 Mix equal parts of:
Dijon Dressing (page 162)
Thousand Island Dressing (page 168)

2 Pour over and toss with:
6 cups Iceberg lettuce in bite-sized chunks
1½ cups quartered, peeled tomatoes
¾ cup sliced carrots
¼ cup sliced scallions

Don't miss this delicious combination dressing; keep it in mind as a "planned-over" when you make Dijon and Thousand Island Dressings.

GIBLET FRICASSEE
(BUTTERED NOODLES)
FARMER'S CHOP SUEY
Serves 4

GIBLET FRICASSEE

1 Sauté in 2-quart flameproof casserole:
    1½ pounds chicken gizzards and hearts
in:
    2 tablespoons Chicken Fat (page 173) or butter
Turn to sear on all sides.

2 Add and continue sautéeing for 5 minutes:
    3 cups thinly sliced Vidalia or Bermuda onions

3 Add:
    2 teaspoons Seasoned Salt (page 172)
    2 cups Bordeaux wine
    1 cup chicken broth
      or 1 cup water plus 1 teaspoon chicken base
Cover and simmer for 1½-2 hours or until giblets are tender.

4 Slice gizzards, discarding any tough membrane.

5 Add:
    ¼ cup lemon juice

6 Thicken to desired consistency with:
    Instant blend flour

7 Serve over noodles.

For added richness, you may wish to include some skinned chicken necks at Step 1. (Remove after completing Step 3.)

To make this a complete one-dish meal, add 1 cup each of carrots, celery and mushrooms after first 45 minutes of cooking time.

chickchat
We promised you could use every part of the chicken except the feathers...

FARMER'S CHOP SUEY

1 Prepare and place in salad bowl:
    1 cup tomatoes, peeled, seeded and cut into bite-sized pieces
    ¾ cup sliced radishes
    ¾ cup sliced carrots
    1 cup diced cucumber
    ⅓ cup diced red pepper

2 Thirty minutes before serving, mix generously with:
    Sour Cream Dressing (page 165)

Pass the pepper mill.

To prepare in advance, the vegetables may be cut and stored in individual sandwich bags until 30 minutes before serving.

The Company Way
Decrease tomatoes to ½ cup and use tossed vegetables to fill hollowed out tomatoes, placed on a bed of lettuce.

Stewed Chicken

your chickchat

3

chicken through
the garden

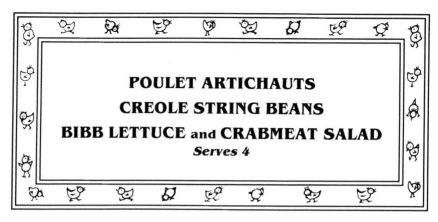

POULET ARTICHAUTS
CREOLE STRING BEANS
BIBB LETTUCE and CRABMEAT SALAD
Serves 4

POULET ARTICHAUTS

1 Place in a single layer, skin side down, in a flameproof au gratin dish:

> **3 pounds fryer parts (breasts, legs, and thighs)**

Brown under broiler, turning legs and thighs to brown all sides. Remove chicken, letting drippings remain in dish.

2 Change oven setting to 350°.

3 Rinse and drain on paper towels:

> **1 7¾-ounce can artichoke bottoms**

Sauté artichoke bottoms in chicken drippings for 2 minutes on each side. Remove from dish and set aside.

4 Sauté for 10 minutes in chicken drippings:

> **18 tiny new potatoes, peeled**

Turn several times until lightly browned. Remove and set aside.

5 Sauté in chicken drippings until they give up their juices:

> **1 pound mushrooms**

Remove and set aside.

6 Deglaze pan with:

> **1 cup dry white wine**
> **1 teaspoon chicken base**
> **½ cup chicken broth or water**

7 Place artichoke bottoms and potatoes in pan, and add:

> **½ cup sliced pimiento**
> **½ cup tiny onions, frozen or fresh**

Cover vegetables with chicken, skin side up.

8 Bake in preheated oven for 45 minutes, basting with pan juices every 15 minutes.

9 Baste once more; thicken pan juices slightly with:

> **Instant blend flour**

10 Add mushrooms and bake 5 minutes more.

Family Way

A less expensive version of this one-dish meal can be prepared by eliminating artichoke bottoms. The wine can be replaced with additional chicken broth.

CREOLE STRING BEANS

1 Cook, according to package directions:
> **2 10-ounce packages frozen French style string beans**

Drain.

2 Combine with:
> **2 cups Creole sauce (below)**

3 When ready to serve, stir in:
> **Half of 1 chopped hard-boiled egg**

Reheat.

4 Garnish with remaining chopped egg.

CREOLE SAUCE

1 Sauté until onion is transparent:
> **1 tablespoon chopped onion**
> **3 tablespoons chopped red and green pepper**

in:
> **2 tablespoons butter**

Remove with slotted spoon and set aside.

2 Stir in:
> **2 tablespoons flour**

Cook over medium heat, stirring frequently, until flour is lightly browned.

3 Stir in gradually to prevent lumps:
> **1 15-ounce can tomato sauce**
> **½ pound young okra, sliced**

4 Add:
> **Sautéed onions and peppers**
> **½ teaspoon salt**
> **1 teaspoon sugar**
> **⅛ teaspoon cayenne pepper**
> **¼ teaspoon freshly ground pepper**
> **¼ teaspoon paprika**
> **¼ cup chopped green olives with pimiento** *

5 Bring to boil and simmer over medium heat for 10 minutes.

* *The variety labelled Salad Olives is a less expensive substitute for whole olives.*

This sauce is also excellent over leftover chicken, turkey, or shrimp. Make several measures, and freeze it in pint containers to have on hand when leftovers present themselves!

67

BIBB LETTUCE and CRABMEAT SALAD

1 Wash, drain, trim and place upside down on a paper towel in plastic bag to dry:
   4 small heads bibb lettuce

2 Drain on paper towel:
   1 6½-ounce can jumbo lump backfin crabmeat

3 Slice a piece off the core of each head, so the lettuce will sit flat. Spread leaves of lettuce and place on plate.

4 Arrange in lettuce leaves:
   12 cherry tomatoes

5 Distribute drained crab throughout lettuce.

6 Serve with:
   Rémoulade Dressing (page 168)
   or
   Dijon Dressing (page 162)_

The Company Way
This is sensational made with *fresh* lump backfin crabmeat!

**CHICKEN FLORENTINE with
SAUCE CHORON**

PARSLEY BUTTER NEW POTATOES

PEA POD and RED CABBAGE SALAD
Serves 4

CHICKEN FLORENTINE with SAUCE CHORON

1 Melt:
   3 tablespoons butter
with:
   2 cloves garlic, cut in half
Set aside for 30 minutes; then remove garlic.

2 Steam until wilted:
   1 pound spinach

3 Drain well. Season to taste with:
   Salt
   Freshly ground pepper
   2 tablespoons butter

4 Using 1 tablespoon of garlic butter, sauté in skillet:
   1 pound mushrooms, sliced
   3 tablespoons minced leeks
Remove from skillet and set aside.

5 Add 1 tablespoon garlic butter to skillet; sauté until tender
   (about 3 minutes):
   ⅓ cup diced sweet red pepper
Remove from skillet and set aside.

6 Using remaining garlic butter, sauté 2 minutes on each side:
   4 chicken breasts, skinned, boned, and halved
Remove chicken from skillet and set aside.

7 Drain mushrooms and peppers, adding juices to skillet.

8 Deglaze skillet with:
   ¾ cup dry white wine

9 Return chicken to pan. Cover. Simmer over medium heat for
   10 minutes, turning every 3 minutes.

10 Add peppers and mushrooms, cooking until heated through.

→

11 If more than 1 tablespoon liquid remains, thicken with a few sprinkles:
  Instant blend flour
12 Serve over seasoned spinach topped with Sauce Choron. Pass extra sauce.

May be prepared in advance through Step 5.

SAUCE CHORON   *Makes 1 cup*

1 Simmer until 1 tablespoon liquid remains:
  2 tablespoons dry white wine
  2 tablespoons Tarragon Vinegar (page 174)
  2 teaspoons minced shallots or onions
2 Place above ingredients in food processor in OFF position with:
  ¼ cup (3) egg yolks
  Using steel knife, process with one ON/OFF pulse.
3 Heat to boiling:
  1 stick sweet butter
4 With processor running, add butter in a steady stream. This should take about a minute.
5 With processor OFF, add:
  3 tablespoons tomato paste at room temperature
  Process with one ON/OFF pulse.
6 Season to taste.
7 If desired, add:
  Chopped parsley
8 Keep warm over hot, NOT BOILING, water until ready to serve.

PARSLEY BUTTER NEW POTATOES

1 Boil until tender:
  12-16 small red new potatoes
  Drain; cool and peel.
2 Season with:
  Melted butter
  Salt
  Freshly ground pepper
3 Place in serving bowl and sprinkle with:
  2 tablespoons chopped fresh parsley

PEA POD and RED CABBAGE SALAD

1 Boil in 1-quart saucepan:
  ½ cup water
  ½ teaspoon salt

2 Cook in boiling salted water for 2 minutes, stirring frequently:
  6 ounces frozen or fresh Chinese pea pods
Avoid overcooking to retain crispness.

3 Drain thoroughly and marinate several hours or overnight in the refrigerator in:
  ⅓ cup Red Wine Vinegar and Oil Dressing (page 162)

4 Place undrained peapods in salad bowl and toss with:
  3 cups thinly sliced red cabbage
  ½ teaspoon salt
  1 teaspoon celery seed (optional)
  ¼ cup corn relish
You may wish to add a little more dressing and some freshly ground pepper.

chickchat
Pea Pod and Red Cabbage Salad is an original — crunchy and colorful! This is a great DO-AHEAD salad.

CHICKEN THROUGH THE GARDEN

LETTUCE WEDGES with BLUE CHEESE DRESSING (page 166)

Serves 6

CHICKEN THROUGH THE GARDEN

1 Lightly brown:
   1 cup frozen chopped onion (¾ cup fresh)

2 In 14" flameproof serving pan melt:
   1 tablespoon chicken fat or oil

3 Remove skin from:
   12 serving pieces frying chicken

4 Sprinkle chicken with:
   1½ teaspoons salt
   ¼ teaspoon freshly ground pepper
   ½ teaspoon thyme

5 Sear chicken in skillet with onion. Then push chicken to sides of pan and deglaze pan with:
   ⅓ cup dry vermouth or dry white wine

6 Return chicken to center of skillet and surround with piles of the following vegetables, taking care not to mix them:
   1½ cups zuccini slices, skin on
   1½ cups 1" celery pieces mixed with 1 diced sweet red pepper
   3 cups thinly sliced carrots (⅜")

7 Pour over vegetables and chicken:
   4 cups plum tomatoes packed in tomato purée (chop them a little)

8 Tie in a piece of cheese cloth and place in skillet:
   1 clove garlic
   1 bay leaf
   1 tablespoon chopped fresh basil (1 teaspoon dried)
   12 peppercorns

9 Cover skillet and simmer until chicken is tender, about 50 minutes, or bring to a boil on the stove and bake at 325° for 1 hour.

10 Remove bag of spices.

11 Shift vegetables in skillet to make space for:
  3 cups raw corn kernels mixed with ¼ teaspoon salt
  If using frozen, thaw and drain before adding to skillet.

12 Sprinkle with:
  ¾ cup sliced stuffed olives
  Baste thoroughly with tomatoes and cook 10 minutes more.

13 Tip skillet to one side to collect juices and thicken with:
  Instant blend flour
  Serve in cooking pan.

A covered paella pan is a very attractive pan to cook and serve in. A 14" deep dish pizza pan may also be used (cover tightly with foil.) To use a skillet in the oven, remove handle.

chickchat

Striking to the eye, Chicken Through The Garden is a color wheel created by arranging bright contrasting vegetables around a hub of seasoned chicken. As convenient as it is attractive, it can be cooked *and* served in a paella pan.

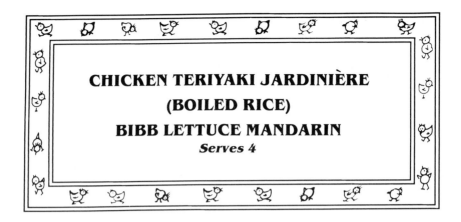

CHICKEN TERIYAKI JARDINIÈRE
(BOILED RICE)
BIBB LETTUCE MANDARIN
Serves 4

CHICKEN TERIYAKI JARDINIÈRE

1 Skin, bone, and cut into finger-size strips:
   2 1-pound chicken breasts

2 Marinate chicken in a plastic bag for 1-2 hours, turning bag occasionally, with:
   2 tablespoons Teriyaki sauce
   ¼ cup sherry

3 Place in base of steamer and bring to a boil:
   2 cups chicken broth
      or 2 cups water plus 2 teaspoons chicken base
   2 tablespoons chopped leeks

4 In basket, steam for 10 minutes:
   ¾ cup tiny frozen onions
   1½ cups new potatoes, 1″ diameter

5 Continue steaming, adding to basket:
   2 cups carrots, cut into matchstick pieces

6 After 5 minutes, place marinated chicken in basket, allowing marinade to drain into steamer base. Also add:
   1 cup red peppers, cut into matchstick pieces
   2 cups zucchini, cut into matchstick pieces
   2 cups broccoli, cut into buds
   2 cups cauliflower, cut into buds
   Steam for 10 minutes.

7 Thicken remaining liquid from steamer base with:
   Instant blend flour
   Place chicken and vegetables into serving dish and toss gently with thickened sauce.

8 Sprinkle with:
   2 tablespoons chopped fresh parsley

The Company Way
Add to the steamer basket for the last 5 minutes:
> **1 cup Chinese peapods**
> **½ cup sliced bamboo shoots**
> **¼ cup sliced water chestnuts**

To prepare in advance, slice chicken and vegetables and refrigerate.

BIBB LETTUCE MANDARIN

1 Remove outside leaves and a small slice from the end of:
> **4 small heads bibb lettuce**

Place on individual salad plates and spread leaves open.

2 Tuck in among the lettuce leaves:
> **Mandarin orange slices, well drained**

3 Sprinkle with:
> **Pumpkin seeds**

4 Pass:
> **Honey Lime Fruit Salad Dressing (page 169)**

chickchat
A pleasant light supper with a spring flair.

75

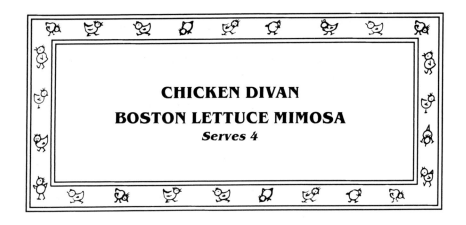

CHICKEN DIVAN
BOSTON LETTUCE MIMOSA
Serves 4

CHICKEN DIVAN

1 Preheat oven to 350°.

2 Steam 10-15 minutes or until tender crisp:
**½ pound fresh broccoli, cut into 5" florets
or 1 10-ounce box frozen**

3 Sauté:
½ pound mushrooms, sliced
in:
2 tablespoons butter

4 Cook according to package directions, substituting chicken broth for water:
**1 10-ounce package frozen peas
1½ cups chicken broth
or 1½ cups water plus 1½ teaspoons chicken base**
Drain peas, reserving chicken broth.

5 Add mushroom juice to chicken broth and boil for 5 minutes.

6 Thicken broth with:
2 tablespoons instant blend flour
Stir in:
**1 tablespoon freshly grated Parmesan cheese
1 2-ounce jar sliced pimiento**
Mix in peas.

7 Arrange in flameproof serving dish:
8 ounces cooked sliced turkey or chicken breast

8 Cover with:
Half of 4 ounces grated sharp cheddar cheese
In layers, place broccoli, then mushrooms. Finally pour sauce over all.

76

9 Bake in preheated oven until heated through and bubbly.

10 Sprinkle with:

Remaining 2 ounces grated sharp cheddar cheese

11 Return to oven for 5 minutes or until cheese melts.

To prepare a day in advance, follow recipe Steps 2 through 8 and refrigerate. An hour before serving time, remove from refrigerator to bring to room temperature. Then complete recipe.

BOSTON LETTUCE MIMOSA

1 Place in plastic bag:

1 cup beets; cooked, drained, and cut in julienne strips

1 tablespoon Italian Dressing (page 162)

Marinate in refrigerator several hours or overnight.

2 Rinse, drain, and cut in half:

4 artichoke hearts, canned

Marinate in plastic bag several hours or overnight in refrigerator with:

1 tablespoon Italian Dressing

3 Toss marinated vegetables with:

4 cups Boston lettuce, broken into bite-sized pieces

½ cup shredded red cabbage

½ cup chopped celery

¼ cup Italian Dressing

4 Garnish with:

1 hard-boiled egg, finely chopped

Chicken Divan

77

your chickchat

4

chicken in
the orchard

CHICKEN MELBA

CREAMED SPINACH

BIBB LETTUCE with
RASPBERRY VINEGAR DRESSING
Serves 4   **(page 163)**

CHICKEN MELBA

1 Place in plastic bag:
   4 chicken breasts, skinned and split

2 Blend well and pour over chicken:
   ½ teaspoon sugar
   ⅛ teaspoon salt
   ½ teaspoon Dijon mustard
   2 tablespoons Raspberry Vinegar (page 174)
   3 tablespoons oil
   Close bag and shake to coat chicken with marinade.
   Marinate 1 hour, turning occasionally.

   While chicken is marinating, prepare the following sauce:

3 Force through a fine strainer, discarding seeds:
   1 10-ounce package frozen raspberries

4 In a 1-quart saucepan, blend raspberries with:
   ¼ cup jellied cranberry sauce
   Bring to a boil, and cook until cranberry sauce melts.

5 In a small measuring cup, mix together:
   2 tablespoons sugar
   ⅛ teaspoon salt
   1 tablespoon cornstarch

6 Blend well with dry ingredients:
   1 tablespoon marinade
   1 tablespoon water

7 Add cornstarch mixture to cranberry sauce and raspberries.
   Bring to a boil, stirring constantly, over medium heat. Reduce
   heat and simmer 2 minutes, stirring occasionally.

8 Preheat oven to 325°.

9 Remove chicken from marinade and drain on paper towels.
   Reserve marinade.

10 Using a shallow flameproof serving dish large enough to place chicken in a single layer, sear chicken 2 minutes on each side over medium-high heat in:
  2 tablespoons butter

11 Reduce heat to medium, and add:
  2 tablespoons marinade
  Simmer 4 minutes, turning occasionally.

12 Place in dish with chicken:
  8 canned peach halves
  Baste peaches with pan juices.

13 Bake 10 minutes in preheated oven, basting once with pan juices.

14 Spoon hot sauce over chicken, leaving peaches uncovered, and pass remaining sauce.

Raspberry vinegar's delightfully fresh flavor is made by steeping ripe raspberries in white wine vinegar.

To prepare a day in advance, follow recipe through Step 7 and refrigerate.

chickchat
For peach melba lovers, this is dessert for dinner!

CREAMED SPINACH

1 Sauté:
  1 tablespoon chopped shallots
    or 2 teaspoons chopped onion
  in:
  1 tablespoon butter

2 Thaw and squeeze water from:
  2 10-ounce packages frozen chopped spinach
  Place in a 1-quart flameproof serving dish with sautéed shallots.

3 Add and stir until well-blended:
  ¼ teaspoon freshly ground pepper
  2 tablespoons cornstarch
  ½ teaspoon salt

4 Stir in:
  1 cup half & half
  Heat to bubbling, stirring constantly. Reduce heat, and simmer two minutes, stirring occasionally.

May be prepared in advance, covered with plastic wrap, refrigerated, and reheated.

81

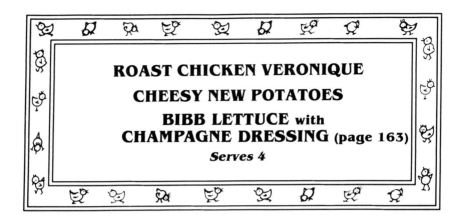

ROAST CHICKEN VERONIQUE

CHEESY NEW POTATOES

BIBB LETTUCE with
CHAMPAGNE DRESSING (page 163)

Serves 4

ROAST CHICKEN VERONIQUE

1 Preheat oven to 450°.

2 Have ready:
>**3 cups seedless green grapes
>(Freezing Grapes, page 175)**

3 Season:
>**1 4-pound fryer**
>inside and out, with:
>**Seasoned Salt (page 172)**

4 Fill cavity of chicken with grapes and place in baking pan. Set aside whatever grapes will not fit in cavity.

5 Sauté:
>**½ pound mushrooms, sliced**
>in:
>**1 tablespoon butter**
>Remove mushrooms with slotted spoon; set aside. Reserve juice.

6 Pour reserved mushroom juice into baking pan with chicken and:
>**¾ cup dry white wine**

7 Place in preheated oven; reduce heat immediately to 325°. Bake 45 minutes, basting twice with pan juices.

8 Place mushrooms and remaining grapes into pan with chicken; continue baking for 15 minutes.

9 Remove chicken from pan; pour juices and grapes from cavity back into pan.

10 Thicken pan juices with:
  Instant blend flour
  (If there is a large amount of liquid in pan, boil for 5 minutes to reduce before thickening.)

11 Season to taste.

To prepare in advance, follow recipe Steps 2-6 and refrigerate.

The Family Way
Substitute orange juice for wine.

CHEESY NEW POTATOES

1 Preheat oven to 325°.

2 Boil until tender:
  ½ pound tiny new potatoes
  Peel.

3 Place in flameproof casserole and toss with:
  2 tablespoons melted butter
  ¼ teaspoon salt
  ⅛ teaspoon freshly ground pepper

4 Bake in preheated oven until heated through.

5 Top with:
  4 ounces shredded Mt. St. Benoit (Canadian) cheese
  (The cheese should be very cold when you shred it.)
  Return to oven until cheese melts.

Pass the pepper mill when serving.

Steps 2 and 3 may be done ahead.

chickchat
These potatoes taste a lot like the popular raclette.

83

CARROT TOP CHICKEN
GREEN RICE
SLICED ROMAINE with
GREEN GODDESS DRESSING (page 167)

Serves 4

CARROT TOP CHICKEN

1 Parboil until just tender:
   2 cups carrots, cut into 1" sections

2 Combine to make glaze:
   6 tablespoons dark brown sugar
   6 tablespoons orange marmalade
   3 tablespoons frozen orange juice concentrate
   3 tablespoons water
   2 tablespoons lemon juice

3 Place in a single layer in a flameproof serving dish:
   3-4 pound fryer, disjointed
   Brown under broiler on all sides; remove from dish. Pour fat out of dish.

4 Season chicken with:
   Seasoned Salt (page 172)

5 Change oven setting to 450°.

6 Deglaze dish with 2 tablespoons glaze.

7 Arrange chicken and carrots attractively in dish. With pastry brush, coat with glaze.

8 Bake in preheated oven for 10 minutes.

9 Turn legs and thighs to crisp all sides. Baste chicken and carrots.

10 Reduce heat to 350°, and continue baking for 15 minutes.

11 Add:
   ½ cup green pepper, sliced in strips
   1½ cups fresh, sliced navel orange
   (To section orange, peel with knife; then slice between membranes to remove sections.)

84

12 Baste. (By basting with just enough to coat, sugar will caramelize making a rich glaze.) Continue baking 20 minutes more, basting two more times.

13 Remove from oven. Sprinkle with:
Chopped fresh parsley

GREEN RICE

1 Preheat oven to 350°.

2 In a 2-quart flameproof serving dish, bring to a boil:
1 tablespoon dried celery leaves
3 tablespoons butter
1½ cups chicken broth
½ teaspoon salt
¼ teaspoon freshly ground pepper

3 Stir in:
¾ cup brown rice
Cover with tight lid and bake in preheated oven for 1¼ hours.

4 While rice is baking, cook, cool and squeeze dry:
2 10-ounce packages frozen chopped spinach

5 Stir into spinach:
¼ teaspoon freshly grated nutmeg
¼ cup snipped chives (1 tablespoon dried)
⅓ cup coarsely chopped water chestnuts
2 tablespoons chopped parsley (2 teaspoons dried)
¼ cup pine nuts
¼ cup sliced pimiento
Combine rice and spinach, stirring gently to blend.

This rice can be served immediately or prepared ahead and reheated at 325°. If reheating, stir after 15 minutes and continue heating until piping hot.

chickchat

The combination of oranges and greens, and the blend of sweet and tart flavors go together to make this menu a study in contrast.

CHICKEN CALVADOS
SESAME POTATOES
(STEAMED ASPARAGUS with BUTTER and LEMON PEPPER)
LETTUCE WEDGES with GORGONZOLA DRESSING (page 166)
Serves 6

CHICKEN CALVADOS

1 Preheat oven to 325°.

2 Set aside to bring to room temperature:
2 tablespoons sour cream

3 Sauté in a single layer for ½ minute on each side:
3 cups Granny Smith apples, cut into ½" slices
in:
2 tablespoons butter
Remove apples from skillet and place in a shallow flameproof serving dish.

4 Sprinkle:
3 1-pound chicken breasts; skinned, boned, and halved
with:
Seasoned Salt (page 172)

5 Add to skillet:
2 tablespoons butter
Sear chicken breasts on both sides in butter. Remove from skillet and place in single layer over apples.

6 Deglaze skillet with:
3 tablespoons Calvados
½ cup dry white wine
¼ cup frozen apple juice concentrate
Pour over chicken and apples, basting each piece to coat.

7 Tie in cheesecloth and slide under chicken breasts:
1 cinnamon stick
4 whole cloves

8 Bake in preheated oven for 20-25 minutes, basting three times.

9 Remove from oven and take out bag of spices. Tip dish to collect pan juices and thicken with:
Instant blend flour

10 Stir sour cream into sauce. Baste chicken with sauce.

11 If desired, place under broiler for 2 minutes to brown further.

12 Sprinkle with:
   1 tablespoon chopped fresh parsley

Calvados du Pays d'Auge Boulard has an especially rich apple flavor and is considered particularly good for cooking.

chickchat

Chicken Calvados is adapted from a specialty of the house of "The Outside Inn," a fine French restaurant in the Algarve in Portugal, run by an English couple who had moved there fully intending to retire.

SESAME POTATOES

1 Preheat oven to 350°.

2 Have ready:
   ¼ cup Clarified Butter, melted (page 173)

3 Prepare:
   4 cups diced peeled potatoes
   Blot dry without rinsing.

4 Sauté:
   ¾ cup frozen chopped onion (⅔ cup fresh)
   in:
   2 tablespoons Clarified Butter

5 Coat a 9" nonstick pie plate (or skillet with handle removed) with:
   2 teaspoons vegetable oil

6 Make 3 layers of potatoes in greased pan. Sprinkle first 2 layers with:
   ½ of sautéed onion
   2 teaspoons Clarified Butter
   Seasoned Salt (page 172)
   Top the third layer with:
   2 teaspoons Clarified Butter
   Seasoned Salt

7 Cover potatoes with aluminum foil, double thickness, and place a heavy oven-safe pan on top of foil. Press down firmly on the pan to mold the potatoes to the baking dish. Leaving pan on, cook the potatoes over medium high heat for 15 minutes. (If your pan isn't heavy, weight it down.)

8 Uncover potatoes and sprinkle with:
   1 tablespoon sesame seed

9 Bake in preheated oven for 30 minutes. Raise oven temperature to 475° and continue baking for 15 minutes or until potatoes are nicely browned.

PLUM GOOD CHICKEN
RICE PILAF
ASPARAGUS VINAIGRETTE
Serves 4

PLUM GOOD CHICKEN

1 Bring to a boil in small saucepan:
9 Italian prune plums, finely chopped
1 tablespoon oil
½ cup corn syrup*
1 cup plum wine
½ cup chutney sauce

2 Stir in, using wire whisk to prevent lumps from forming:
1 tablespoon instant blend flour

3 In a shallow flameproof serving dish, brown under the broiler on both sides:
8 serving pieces frying chicken
Drain off fat.

4 Change oven setting to 325°.

5 Dip chicken in plum sauce to coat and place in dish. Bake 40 minutes in preheated oven, turning and basting with additional sauce every 15 minutes.

6 Stir into remaining sauce and simmer 10 minutes:
¼ cup currants
Pour over chicken when ready to serve.

*Coat measuring cup with the oil before using it for the corn syrup; the corn syrup will then pour right out.

chickchat
Served with a glass of real plum wine, this is an elegant menu for Saturday night.

RICE PILAF

1 Sauté:
   ⅓ cup frozen chopped onion (¼ cup fresh chopped)
   in:
   4 tablespoons butter

2 Stir in until coated with butter:
   1 cup raw rice

3 Add:
   ⅛ teaspoon freshly ground pepper
   ½ teaspoon salt
   ⅛ teaspoon thyme
   ¼ teaspoon Lemon Zest (page 175)
   1 small bay leaf
   2 tablespoons fresh lemon juice
   1½ cups chicken broth, heated to boiling
   or 1½ cups water plus 1½ teaspoons chicken base

4 Place on heat-diffusing pad: bring to a boil and stir. Cover pan
   and cook over low heat for 25 minutes without stirring. Allow
   to stand 10 minutes after cooking.

5 Remove bay leaf and add:
   1 10-ounce package frozen peas, cooked according
   to package directions
   ¼ cup chopped water chestnuts
   2 tablespoons chopped fresh parsley
   2 teaspoons dill weed

May be prepared in advance and reheated in oven.

The Company Way
At Step 5 add 1 9-ounce package frozen artichoke hearts, cooked
according to directions on package.

ASPARAGUS VINAIGRETTE

1 Steam until tender crisp:
   4-6 stalks asparagus per person
   Refresh under cold water, drain, and refrigerate, covered, until
   time to assemble salad.

2 Arrange on bed of:
   Shredded lettuce

3 Drizzle with:
   Avocado Vinaigrette Dressing (page 165)

POLLO SERPICO
CORN and BROCCOLI PUDDING
CELERY ROOT RÉMOULADE
Serves 4

POLLO SERPICO

1 Preheat oven to 325°.

2 Skin, bone, and halve:
   4 chicken breasts

3 Combine and sprinkle on chicken breasts:
   ½ teaspoon salt
   ¼ teaspoon freshly ground pepper
   4 teaspoons Parmesan cheese

4 Roll breasts and fasten with toothpicks.

5 Combine:
   ¼ cup cracker crumbs
   ½ teaspoon thyme
   ¼ cup Parmesan cheese
   ¼ teaspoon freshly ground pepper
   ½ teaspoon salt

6 Roll chicken breasts in crumb mixture. Chill 1 hour.

7 Melt in flameproof serving dish:
   2 tablespoons butter
   Place chicken in butter, turning once to coat.

8 Drain, reserving syrup:
   2 17-ounce cans whole peeled apricots

9 Combine:
   ¼ cup dry vermouth
   3 tablespoons reserved apricot syrup
   or 1½ tablespoons reserved apricot syrup
   plus 1½ tablespoons apricot brandy
   Sprinkle over chicken.

10 Bake in preheated oven for 35 minutes, basting every 10 minutes with pan juices.

11 If necessary, thicken pan juices with:
   Instant blend flour

12 Arrange apricots among chicken pieces. Baste with pan juices.

13 Bake 15 minutes longer.

The Company Way
Warm 3 tablespoons apricot brandy slightly in ladle over burner. When ready to serve, ignite it with a match and pour it flaming over chicken.

chickchat

" . . . In one corner, beneath a huge tapestry of a romantic nude surrounded by cherubs and a Tiffany lamp suspended from the ceiling, there is a round, white marble table which in a pinch can seat four. Like most of the other furnishings in the room — a maple chest, a small sofa, and a big armchair with a footstool — they were picked up by Serpico in secondhand shops around the city. In another corner is a kitchenette, partially hidden by a carved Indian screen, where he expertly prepares such dishes as *chicken breasts with apricots...*" *****

* Excerpt from *Serpico, The Cop Who Defied The System* — by Peter Maas

CORN and BROCCOLI PUDDING

1 Cook according to package directions, for minimum time suggested:

> **1 10-ounce package frozen broccoli spears**

Drain thoroughly and season with:

> **2 teaspoons melted butter**
> **Salt and freshly ground pepper to taste**

Arrange in single layer in well greased flameproof casserole.

2 Combine:
>**4 beaten egg yolks**
>**2 tablespoons melted butter**
>**1 12-ounce can corn and peppers, well drained**
>**2 14½-ounce cans cream style corn**

3 Preheat oven to 325°.

4 Beat until stiff:
>**4 egg whites**
>**½ teaspoon salt**
>**¼ teaspoon freshly ground pepper**

Stir corn mixture and fold in egg whites.

5 Pour over broccoli. Sprinkle with:
>**1 tablespoon Parmesan cheese**

6 Bake in preheated oven for 40 minutes or until custard is set.

If you are in a rush, add whole eggs, salt and pepper at Step 2. It won't have the light soufflé-like consistency, but will taste swell.

For people who like highly seasoned vegetables, add 1-2 tablespoons chopped chili peppers at Step 2.

During the corn season, substitute for canned corn and peppers:
>**1 cup raw corn, scraped from the cob**
>**1 tablespoon chopped sweet red pepper**
>**1 tablespoon chopped green pepper.**

CELERY ROOT RÉMOULADE

1 Peel and cut into julienne strips:
>**1⅓ cups celery root**

2 Sprinkle with:
>**Lemon juice**

3 Toss with:
>**Rémoulade Dressing (page 168)**

4 Divide into individual servings and serve on lettuce leaves.

5 Garnish with any of the following:
>**Cherry tomatoes**
>**Capers**
>**Chopped walnuts**

This dressing is also good with:
Raw cauliflower buds
Raw asparagus
Heart of palm, sliced
Raw mushrooms, sliced

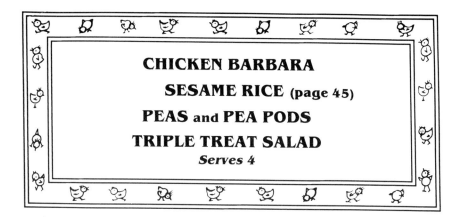

CHICKEN BARBARA

SESAME RICE (page 45)

PEAS and **PEA PODS**

TRIPLE TREAT SALAD

Serves 4

CHICKEN BARBARA

1 Season:
   4 chicken breasts, halved
with:
   Seasoned Salt (page 172)

2 In shallow flameproof serving dish, large enough to place chicken in a single layer, broil chicken to brown lightly on all sides.

3 Pour off fat. Place chicken, skin side up, in dish.

4 Change oven setting to 325°.

5 In small saucepan, boil to reduce to ½ cup:
   ¾ cup frozen apple juice concentrate

6 Add to apple juice:
   ½ teaspoon chicken base

7 Place in dish with chicken:
   4 medium nectarines, seeded and quartered
Pour apple juice over all.

8 Bake in preheated oven 40 minutes, basting every 15 minutes.

9 While chicken is baking, sauté:
   ⅓ cup cashews
in:
   2 teaspoons butter

10 After baking chicken, drain pan juices into a small saucepan. Boil to reduce to 1¾ cups.

11 Thicken with:
   Instant blend flour
Pour thickened gravy over chicken and fruit. Sprinkle with sautéed cashews.

93

chickchat

An original, Chicken Barbara is a proven smash at buffet dinners. Affordable company fare!

PEAS and PEA PODS

1 Heat in skillet:
1 tablespoon oil

2 Sauté in oil until transparent:
2 tablespoons chopped shallots

3 Add to skillet and stir-fry 1 minute:
2 10-ounce packages frozen tiny peas
12 ounces fresh or frozen pea pods
Drain.

4 Season with:
Salt
Pepper
Butter

5 Stir in:
1 4-ounce jar sliced pimiento
¼ cup sliced water chestnuts

TRIPLE TREAT SALAD

1 For each salad, prepare a bed of:
Shredded romaine

2 On the romaine, place small scoops (⅓ cup) of each of the following:
Dilled Cucumbers
Marinated Radishes
Tomatoes in Guacamole

DILLED CUCUMBERS

1 Peel and cut into ¼″ slices:
6 cups cucumbers

2 Sprinkle with:
1 tablespoon salt
Place in plastic bag and let stand 1-2 hours or longer, turning occasionally. Rinse thoroughly and drain in colander, or dry in salad spinner.

3 Mix with:
1 measure Sour Cream Dressing (page 165;
follow recipe instructions omitting salt)

4 Sprinkle with:
1 tablespoon dill weed

94

MARINATED RADISHES

1 Wash, dry and cut into ⅛″ slices, desired amount of:
Red or white radishes

2 Place in plastic bag and coat with:
Red Wine Vinegar and Oil dressing (page 162)

3 Close bag and refrigerate several hours, turning bag several times.

The color of red radishes tends to run after about 12 hours.

TOMATOES in GUACAMOLE

1 Toss:
1 cup tomatoes; peeled, cubed, and drained
with:
½ cup Guacamole Dressing (page 169)

Pullet

95

CHERRY CHICKEN

RED CABBAGE and APPLES

BOSTON LETTUCE with PIMIENTO DRESSING

Serves 4

CHERRY CHICKEN

1 Brown under broiler in a flameproof serving dish, large enough to place in a single layer:

4 chicken breasts, halved

2 Remove from oven; change oven setting to 325°.

3 Season with:

Seasoned Salt (page 172)

4 Remove chicken from dish; pour off fat.

5 Deglaze pan with:

1 cup chicken broth
or 1 cup water plus 1 teaspoon chicken base

Pour into small saucepan.

6 Add to broth:

¾ cup tiny onions
3 tablespoons honey
2 tablespoons sugar
1 cinnamon stick
½ teaspoon ginger
3 tablespoons lemon juice
½ teaspoon lemon zest (Frozen Lemon Peels, page 175)
1 tablespoon cornstarch
¼ teaspoon Dijon mustard
1 20-ounce bag frozen sweet cherries; coarsely chop 1 cup of these

Simmer for 10 minutes; stir constantly while mixture thickens, and then occasionally to prevent sticking.

7 Dip each piece of chicken in sauce to coat on all sides. Return chicken pieces to flameproof dish.

8 Pour remaining liquid part of sauce over chicken, reserving cherries. Discard cinnamon stick.

9 Bake in preheated oven for 20 minutes, brushing with sauce every 5 minutes.

10 Add reserved cherries and continue baking 5 minutes longer.

The Company Way
Warm 2 tablespoons Cherry Heering in ladle over burner. When ready to serve, ignite with a match and pour over chicken.

RED CABBAGE and APPLES

1 Preheat oven to 350°.

2 In 2-quart flameproof casserole, sauté:
    ½ cup frozen chopped onions (⅓ cup fresh)
in:
    2 tablespoons bacon fat

3 Add:
    ⅔ cup red wine vinegar
Boil to reduce one half.

4 Add:
    ⅓ cup brown sugar
    1 teaspoon salt
    ⅛ teaspoon grated nutmeg
    ½ teaspoon lemon pepper

5 Stir in:
    3 pounds red cabbage, cored and shredded
    2 cups peeled, sliced tart apples (Granny Smith,
      Stayman Winesap, Rome beauty)
    1 cup white raisins

6 Tie in cheese cloth and place in center of cabbage:
    2 cloves
    1 small bay leaf

7 Cover and bake in preheated oven for 1½ hours.

This dish is excellent made a day or two ahead and reheated. Freeze any leftovers.

BOSTON LETTUCE with PIMIENTO DRESSING

1 Toss:
    6 cups Boston lettuce
with:
    Pimiento Dressing (page 162)

2 Sprinkle with:
    1 tablespoon chopped fresh chives
    2 tablespoons chopped green olives
    ½ cup croutons

chickchat
"A Study in Scarlet"

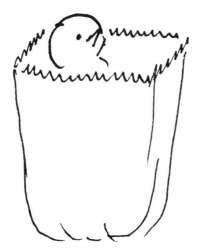

it's in the bag!

it's convenient !

Excellent for cooking poultry, meats, fruits, vegetables,
and for poaching fish.
Marinate and cook in the same bag.
Prepare food ahead; refrigerate or freeze in the bag until
time to cook.
Self-basting!
Perfect browning every time!
No oven spatter!
Easy clean-up!
Available in several sizes!

it's economical !

Bag cooking shortens cooking time.
The moist heat tenderizes connective tissue so you can
buy less tender cuts of meat.

it's perfect for chicken !

Bag cooking produces a moist and tender product.
It preserves nutrients.
Minimal evaporation results in an abundance of gravy.

BAG ROASTED CHICKEN with HARVEST DRESSING

ORANGE RHUBARB COMPOTE

Serves 6

BAG ROASTED CHICKEN with HARVEST DRESSING

1 Preheat oven to 275°.

2 Cut into ¾" squares and spread out on a cookie sheet:
  5 ounces (3 cups) white bread
  Dry in preheated oven for 15 minutes. After removing bread, reset oven to 350°.

3 Sauté:
  ½ cup finely chopped carrots
  in:
  2 tablespoons Chicken Fat (page 173) or oil

4 Add and continue sautéing over medium heat for 8 minutes to wilt:
  1½ cups diced celery
  1 cup frozen chopped onion
  1 cup diced zucchini

5 Combine vegetables and bread in a 3-quart mixing bowl. Stir in:
  ½ cup chopped celery leaves
  1 cup diced apple (Stayman Winesaps, Granny Smith, Rome Beauties or Cortlands)

6 Blend well, adding water gradually:
  1½ teaspoons chicken base
  ½ cup water

7 Stir in:
  1 beaten egg
  ¼ teaspoon pepper
  1 tablespoon chopped fresh parsley (1 teaspoon dried)
  ½ teaspoon poultry seasoning

8 Dust cavities of
   1 5-pound chicken
or:
   2 3-pound chickens
with:
   Seasoned Salt (page 172)
9 Fill with preceeding stuffing. If there is extra stuffing, bake in a casserole with some wings and necks on top to add flavor.
10 To prevent sticking to bag and to facilitate browning, brush chicken with:
   2 teaspoons oil
11 Place in cooking bag:
   1 tablespoon flour
12 Place chicken in bag, close with twister and place in 2" deep pan. Cut six ½" slits in top of bag.
13 Bake in preheated oven for 1½ hours.
14 Remove from oven; set oven temperature to broil.
15 Cut one corner of the bag. Pour gravy through cut into a transparent container.
16 Cut bag open and pull carefully away from chicken.
17 If you wish to brown underneath side of chicken, place, breast side down, on a stainless steel serving platter. Broil until brown.
18 Skim grease from gravy. Thicken with:
   Instant blend flour
19 Season gravy to taste. If desired for color, add:
   A few drops Kitchen Bouquet

Steps 1-8 can be done in advance, but the chicken must not be stuffed until you are ready to bake it.

ORANGE RHUBARB COMPOTE

1 Preheat oven to 350°.
2 Place in cooking bag:
   4 cups fresh rhubarb cut into 1" pieces
   1 cup peeled and sliced navel orange
   ⅓ cup golden raisins
   1 stick cinnamon
3 Mix together and pour over fruit:
   ½-¾ cup sugar
   1 tablespoon flour
4 Close bag with twister. Place in 2" deep pan. Cut six ½" slits in top of bag.
5 Bake in preheated oven for 40 minutes. Remove cinnamon stick. Chill before serving.

Freezes well.   **101**

IN-THE-BAG CHICKEN
GUACAMOLE SALAD
Serves 4

IN-THE-BAG CHICKEN

1 Preheat oven to 350°.

2 Remove visible fat from a:
    3-4 pound chicken
Brush skin of chicken with:
    Oil or melted butter (optional)

3 Season cavity with:
    ¼ teaspoon salt
    ¼ teaspoon pepper
    1 tablespoon frozen chopped onion
    2 tablespoons chopped celery leaves

4 Place in cooking bag:
    1 tablespoon flour
Place bag in 2″ deep pan.

5 Mix together:
    ⅔ cup white rice
    ⅓ cup dry white wine
    ⅛ teaspoon thyme
    1 teaspoon salt
    ¼ teaspoon pepper
Heap moistened rice in center bottom of cooking bag.

6 Cover rice with:
    ½ cup frozen chopped onion (⅓ cup fresh)
    3 tablespoons chopped fresh parsley (1 tablespoon dried)
    1 cup fresh chopped celery leaves
    1 cup chopped celery
    ½ pound mushrooms, sliced
Vegetables can spread out, but rice *must* remain in a heap in the center of the bag.

7 Place chicken in bag on top of vegetables. Pour in:
   ⅔ cup dry white wine

8 Fasten bag with twister. Cut six ½″ slits in top of bag. Place bag in 2″ deep pan.

9 Bake in preheated oven for 1 hour.

To prepare in advance, follow recipe Steps 2-8 and refrigerate until ready to bake. Or follow Steps 2-8 and freeze; thaw before baking.

The Family Way
Substitute chicken broth for wine.

---

chickchat
"Look Ma, No pans!!!" This is a complete meal in a bag.

GUACAMOLE SALAD

1 Each individual salad requires:
   ¾″ slice of head lettuce
   Sliced tomato to cover

2 Top with:
   Guacamole Dressing (page 169)
   1 teaspoon chopped bacon, crisp
   1 teaspoon chopped walnuts

Career Chicken

103

CHICKEN MARENGO

SHRIMP and CAULIFLOWER RÉMOULADE
Serves 4

CHICKEN MARENGO

1 Preheat oven to 350°.

2 Mix the following ingredients and pour into cooking bag:
   1½ cups drained chopped Italian plum tomatoes, fresh or canned, plus 2 tablespoons reserved juice
   ½ cup raw rice
   ⅔ cups dry white wine
   1 tablespoon melted butter or margarine
   ¼ teaspoon pepper
   2 teaspoons fresh chopped basil (½ teaspoon dried)
   1½ teaspoons salt
   ¼ teaspoon thyme
   2 tablespoons chopped fresh parsley (2 teaspoons dried)
   ½ small clove garlic, pressed
   1 cup small whole frozen onions
   2 cups sliced mushrooms
   ¼ cup chopped fresh celery leaves (1 tablespoon dry)
   ½ cup chopped carrots
   1 cup sliced fresh sweet red pepper
   1 tablespoon flour

3 Place bag in 2" deep pan that is slightly larger than the bag.

4 Place in 1 layer, completely covering sauce:
   8 pieces of frying chicken, skin removed

5 Close bag with twist tie. Make six ½" slits in top of bag.

6 Bake in preheated oven for 1¼ hours.

To prepare in advance, follow recipe Steps 2-6 and refrigerate or freeze until ready to bake. Freeze flat for faster thawing; thaw before baking. Or, cook ahead, refrigerate, and reheat at serving time.

Originally created for Napoleon after the Battle of Marengo, this dish is traditionally served with shrimp. (You'll find the shrimp in the salad.) Updated for today's chef with instructions for "no-pans" use of cooking bags.

SHRIMP and CAULIFLOWER RÉMOULADE

1 Cook in boiling water 1½ minutes:
   ½ pound snap peas
   Drain and refresh with ice water.

2 Cook in boiling water 3-5 minutes:
   2 cups fresh cauliflower buds
   Drain and refresh with ice water.

3 Dry vegetables thoroughly.

4 Marinate in refrigerator several hours or overnight in:
   ¼ cup Rémoulade Dressing (page 168)

5 Toss vegetables with:
   ½ pound cooked tiny shrimp

6 Make individual servings, placing vegetables and shrimp on a bed of:
   Shredded romaine

7 Garnish with:
   12 cherry tomatoes

8 Sprinkle with:
   2 tablespoons snipped fresh chives
   Sunflower seeds
   Alfalfa sprouts

9 Pass additional dressing.

The Family Way
This salad is also very good without the shrimp.

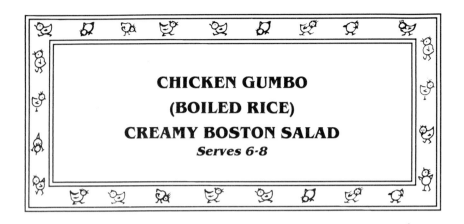

CHICKEN GUMBO
(BOILED RICE)
CREAMY BOSTON SALAD
Serves 6-8

CHICKEN GUMBO

1 Preheat oven to 350°.

2 Season:
   1 4-pound roasting chicken
inside and out with:
   Salt
   Freshly ground pepper

3 Remove visible fat from open end of cavity.

4 Place in cavity:
   1 medium onion, quartered
   1 bay leaf
   ½ cup celery leaves

5 Place in cooking bag:
   1 tablespoon flour
Place chicken in bag. Close bag with twister; place bag in 2" deep pan; make six ½" slits in top of bag.

6 Bake chicken in preheated oven for 1¾ hours. (See Step 14 for instructions for removing.)

7 While chicken is baking, wash quickly under cold running water:
   1 pound young okra
Drain; slice into ⅜" slices, discarding tip and stem ends.

8 Cook in boiling water until tender:
   1½ cups carrots, peeled and sliced into ⅜" slices

9 Fry until crisp:
   6 slices bacon, cut into ¼" strips
Remove with slotted spoon and drain on paper towels. Set aside.

10 Sauté okra in bacon fat over medium heat until tender, about 10 minutes.

106

11 Add to skillet:
    1 cup frozen chopped onion
      or 1 medium onion, chopped
    ⅔ cup diced red bell pepper (½" dice)
Continue sautéing for 15 minutes.

12 Add to skillet:
    2¼ cups chopped, drained tomatoes (#2 can);
      reserve juice.

13 Stir in:
    ½ teaspoon pepper
    1 teaspoon salt
    ¼ teaspoon thyme
    2 teaspoons Worcestershire Sauce

14 Remove chicken from oven, and let stand in bag for 15 minutes.

15 Cut corner of bag; pour off broth into a 4-cup measure. Skim fat; add enough reserved tomato juice to make 4 cups.

16 Melt in skillet:
    3 tablespoons butter
Over low heat, stir in thoroughly and quickly:
    2½ tablespoons flour
Raising heat to medium, continue stirring intermittently until roux is rich tan.

17 Gradually mix 1 cup chicken broth mixture into roux.

18 In a flameproof serving pot, mix roux, remaining stock, tomato mixture, and drained cooked carrots.

19 Remove chicken from bone and cut into 1½" strips. Stir into soup.

20 At the last moment, add:
    1 tablespoon Gumbo filé
Let come to boiling point and remove from stove. DO NOT BOIL!

21 Sprinkle with chopped bacon.

CREAMY BOSTON SALAD

1 Wash well, trim, and drain on paper towels or in salad spinner:
    3-4 small heads Boston lettuce

2 Arrange lettuce on individual plates with:
    9-12 cherry tomatoes

3 Top with:
    Cucumber Dressing (page 165)
    Croutons

**BRUNSWICK STEW
HOT SPINACH SALAD
BLUEBERRY YEAST MUFFINS**
Serves 6

BRUNSWICK STEW

1 Preheat oven to 350°.

2 Wash and drain:
    1 4-pound chicken

3 Sauté:
    4 strips bacon
    2 cups frozen chopped onion (1½ cups fresh)

4 Place in cooking bag:
    1 tablespoon flour

5 Remove bacon and onions from skillet with slotted spoon. Place half in cooking bag, the rest in cavity of chicken. Also place in cavity:
    ½ teaspoon Seasoned Salt (page 172)
    ½ cup chopped celery leaves
Place chicken in cooking bag.

6 Pour over chicken:
    4 cups tomatoes, chopped, peeled, and drained.
Close bag; place bag in 2″ deep pan. Make six ½″ slits in top of bag.

7 Bake in preheated oven for 1 hour.

8 Cut corner of bag and pour broth into an 8-cup measure. Chill and remove fat. Add:
    Chicken broth
to make 7 cups.
Stir in:
    2 teaspoons Worcestershire sauce
    ¼ teaspoon freshly ground pepper

9 Remove chicken from bag; let cool. Spoon onions, celery leaves, and bacon from cavity; stir into broth.

108

10 Remove chicken from bone and break into bite-sized chunks, discarding skin and bone.

11 In a 4-quart flameproof dish, mix chicken and broth. Stir in:
> **3 cups frozen lima beans**
Simmer 20 minutes.

12 Stir in:
> **3 cups frozen corn**
Simmer 15 minutes.

13 Thicken with:
> **Instant blend flour**
Correct seasoning.

This dish may be prepared ahead, refrigerated and reheated. (Stir frequently to prevent sticking).

---

chickchat

We visited Colonial Williamsburg on a rainy, cold day. To escape the weather we ducked into an old inn and sat cozily by the fire enjoying Brunswick Stew and freshly baked bread and butter. Delicious!

HOT SPINACH SALAD

1 Sauté until crisp:
> **¼-pound ham fat**
Remove with slotted spoon and drain on paper towels.

2 Sauté in ham drippings until soft:
> **¼ cup sliced scallions (use white and green)**

3 Add to scallions:
> **2 tablespoons fresh lemon juice**
> **½ teaspoon sugar**
> **1 tablespoon salad oil**

4 Pour over:
> **1-pound fresh spinach, broken into bite-sized pieces**
> **½ pound sliced mushrooms**
> **½ cup diced ripe avocado**

5 Season with:
> **Salt**
> **Freshly ground pepper**

6 Top with:
> **Sautéed ham fat**
> **½ cup pickled beets cut into julienne strips**

Pass pepper mill.

BLUEBERRY YEAST MUFFINS *Makes 16 muffins*

1 Mix in 1-cup measure:
   ¼ cup warm water (body temperature)
   ¼ teaspoon ginger
   1 teaspoon sugar
   1 ½-ounce package dry yeast
   Set in a warm place until yeast bubbles. (if yeast fails to bubble, it is inactive. Start over with another package of yeast)

2 Place in food processor with steel knife and blend with two ON/OFF pulses:
   1¾ cup all-purpose flour
   ¼ cup sugar
   ½ teaspoon salt

3 Add and process 1 minute:
   4 tablespoons butter cut into several pieces
   1 large egg

4 Add and process 1 minute:
   Yeast mixture
   6 tablespoons milk
   1 teaspoon vanilla

5 Pour into 1½-quart bowl, cover and let rise 50 minutes in a warm place until doubled in bulk.

6 Preheat oven to 400°.

7 Wash and dry:
   1 cup blueberries

8 Shake to coat in:
   1 tablespoon flour

9 Stir floured blueberries into batter. Add:
   ¾ cup chopped pecans or walnuts

10 Spoon into well greased muffin tins (fill ⅔ full). Let rise 20 minutes in a warm place.

11 Sprinkle each muffin with:
   ½ teaspoon Cinnamon Sugar (page 172)

12 Bake 15-20 minutes in preheated oven. Remove from pans and cool on wire rack.

Yeast muffins freeze well. To reheat, wrap in foil and warm in preheated 450° oven 10 minutes or until thawed. Yeast muffins stay moist longer than the traditional baking powder muffin.

6

chicks 'n' cheese

CHICKEN FONTINA
PEAS and PROSCIUTTO
FRUIT SALAD MELBA
Serves 4

CHICKEN FONTINA

1 Place in a shallow flameproof serving dish:
   8 serving pieces frying chicken
   seasoned with:
   Seasoned Salt (page 172)
   Brown under broiler, turning to brown all sides. Remove chicken from dish; pour off excess fat.

2 Reset oven to 350°.

3 Sauté in same dish:
   1 pound mushrooms, sliced
   adding to skillet:
   1 tablespoon butter
   Remove with slotted spoon; set aside.

4 Deglaze dish with:
   ¾ cup dry white wine

5 Return chicken to baking dish and turn to coat with wine, ending with skin side up.

6 Bake 30 minutes in preheated oven, basting every 10 minutes.

7 Add sautéed mushrooms; bake 5 more minutes.

8 Skim fat from pan juices and thicken with:
   Instant blend flour

9 Lay over chicken:
   4 ounces sliced Danish Fontina cheese (⅛ " slices)

10 Bake 5 minutes to melt cheese.

11 Sprinkle with ¼ cup pine nuts.

The Family Way
For an economical family meal, substitute mozzarella cheese and replace the pine nuts with almonds (or omit them).

112

PEAS and PROSCIUTTO

1 Sauté until lightly browned:
   ⅓ cup chopped shallots
   in:
   2 tablespoons butter

2 Add and continue sautéing for 2 minutes more:
   ⅓ cup slivered prosciutto

3 Cook, drain and season:
   2 10-ounce packages frozen peas

4 Stir in prosciutto mixture.

May be prepared in advance through Step 2.

FRUIT SALAD MELBA

1 Mix in salad bowl:
   1 cup strawberries
   1 cup grapes
   1 cup blueberries
   1 cup peaches or nectarines
   1 tablespoon sugar
   1 tablespoon lemon or lime juice (fresh)

2 Force through a strainer, discarding seeds:
   1 10-ounce box frozen sweetened raspberries

3 Ladle raspberry sauce over each individual serving of fruit.

Can be prepared in advance through Step 2.

CHICKEN PROVOLONE
(GREEN BEANS with PEARL ONIONS)
CAESAR SALAD
Serves 6

CHICKEN PROVOLONE

1 Combine:
>   **3 cups tomato sauce**
>   **2 tablespoons grated Parmesan cheese**
>   **2 tablespoons dry Vermouth**
>   **¼ teaspoon crumbled oregano**
>   **2 teaspoons fresh chopped basil (½ teaspoon dried)**
>   **½ teaspoon sugar**
>   **1 teaspoon chicken base**
>   **Few grinds pepper**
>   **1 clove garlic; peeled, split, on toothpick**

or use:
>   **3 cups Marinara Sauce (page 176)**

Bring to boil and simmer 15 minutes.

2 Preheat oven to 350°.

3 Sauté, turning to sear on all sides:
>   **6 chicken breasts; skinned, boned and halved**

in:
>   **1 tablespoon butter**

Place in shallow flameproof serving dish.

4 Sauté in same skillet:
>   **1 pound sliced mushrooms**

adding:
>   **1 tablespoon butter**

5 Remove garlic from cooked sauce and pour ⅔ sauce over chicken. Stir mushrooms into remaining sauce; reserve.

6 Bake in preheated oven for 30 minutes; turn and baste after 15 minutes.

7 Pour reserved sauce over chicken and continue baking for 10 minutes.

8 Lay over chicken:
   6 ounces sliced Provolone cheese (⅛″ slices)
   Return to oven until cheese melts.

Sauce can be prepared in quantity in advance and frozen.

CAESAR SALAD

1 In large salad bowl, combine:
   4 tablespoons olive oil
   1 tablespoon Tarragon Vinegar (page 174)
   1 tablespoon red wine vinegar
   1 tablespoon garlic vinegar (page 174)
   Oil drained from 1 2-ounce can anchovies
   2 tablespoons lemon juice
   1 teaspoon dry mustard
   ½ teaspoon salt
   Dash tabasco sauce
   Dash Worcestershire sauce
   A few grinds pepper

2 Add to bowl:
   8 cups romaine
   1 medium avocado, diced

3 Boil for 1 minute, remove from shell, and beat with fork:
   1 egg
   Pour over salad. Toss gently, but well.

4 Top each salad with:
   Croutons
   1 anchovy

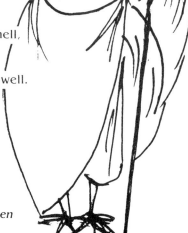

Julius Chicken

115

CHICKEN with PEPPER CHEESE
RATATOUILLE
EVERLASTING COLESLAW
Serves 6

CHICKEN with PEPPER CHEESE

1 Make a double measure of:
    Our Chicken Cordon Bleu (page 118)
with the following change:

2 Replace prosciutto and Swiss cheese with:
    8 ounces hot pepper cheese
Cheese does not have to be thinly sliced; simply divide it
between the chicken breasts.

chickchat
Add ZIP to your chick!

RATATOUILLE

1 Peel and dice:
    1 small eggplant to make 2 cups
Sprinkle with:
    1 teaspoon salt
Place in plastic bag and let sit for 1 hour turning bag
occasionally. Drain.

2 Preheat oven to 350°.

3 Heat in skillet:
    1 tablespoon vegetable or olive oil
Sauté eggplant in oil for about 5 minutes over medium heat
with:
    1 cup frozen chopped onion
    1 clove minced garlic

4 Stir in:

      3 tablespoons tomato paste
      1 tablespoon sugar
      1 teaspoon salt
      1 tablespoon vinegar
      ½ teaspoon oregano
      1 teaspoon dried basil
      1 tablespoon flour

5 Place in cooking bag and add:

      3 cups sliced zucchini
      1 cup green pepper, cut into strips
      1½ cups peeled, diced, drained tomatoes

Turn bag to coat vegetables well.

6 Close bag with twister and make six ½" slits in top. Place in 2" deep pan.

7 Bake in preheated oven for 45 minutes.

Leftovers can be served cold as salad, reheated, or frozen.

EVERLASTING COLESLAW

1 Boil briskly for 4 minutes:

      1 cup vinegar
      1 cup oil
      1 tablespoon salt
      2 teaspoons celery salt
      ¾ cup sugar

2 Add to hot dressing:

      1 medium green pepper, chopped
      1⅓ cups finely chopped white onion

3 Cool dressing and pour over:

      1 3-pound cabbage, shredded

Mix well. Chill several hours or overnight before serving.

Store slaw in a tightly covered jar in the refrigerator. This keeps several months.

Chicken Pox

OUR CHICKEN CORDON BLEU
TOMATO VEGETABLE SCALLOP
MUSHROOM SALAD
Serves 4

OUR CHICKEN CORDON BLEU

1 Chill in plastic bag:
  2 1-pound chicken breasts; split, skinned, and boned

2 Place on a plate:
  1/3 cup Italian Bread Crumbs (page 176)
  Set aside.

3 Place on a plate:
  1/3 cup flour
  Set aside.

4 Pound chilled chicken breasts, one at a time in bag, to
  1/8" thickness, using flat side of a meat tenderizing mallet.

5 Sprinkle with:
  Salt
  White pepper

6 Have ready:
  2 ounces thinly sliced prosciutto
  2 ounces thinly sliced aged Swiss cheese

7 Lay chicken breasts smooth side down. Cover half of each with
  one layer each of prosciutto and cheese, leaving a 1/4" border.
  Fold chicken breasts over. Press seams together.

8 If chicken is moist, pat dry. Using pastry brush, paint seams
  with:
  1 slightly beaten egg
  Add to remaining egg (beating only slightly to avoid forming
  bubbles):
  2 teaspoons milk
  Set aside.

9 Dip chicken in flour, covering completely but lightly. Pat excess
  off.

10 Dip in egg mixture. Use pastry brush to cover *completely.* Let excess drip off.

11 Place in crumb mixture. Cover evenly and completely. Remember to cover edges as well; breading the edges creates a seal that keeps the cheese from running out.

12 Let stand on wire rack for 20 minutes at room temperature.

13 Preheat oven to 400°.

14 Bake in lightly greased dish in preheated oven for 15 minutes, turning once.

15 Remove from oven and serve at once.

The Family Way
Substitute sliced ham, boiled or baked, for prosciutto.

chickchat
"... without even frying!!!"

TOMATO VEGETABLE SCALLOP

1 Preheat oven to 350°.

2 In a 2-quart flameproof casserole, sauté:
½ cup frozen chopped onion (⅓ cup fresh)
⅓ cup diced green pepper
in:
1 tablespoon butter

3 Cook according to package directions, using minimum time suggested:
1 10-ounce package frozen Brussels sprouts
1 9-ounce package frozen artichoke hearts
Drain thoroughly and add to sautéed onion and green pepper.

4 Dip in boiling water and peel:
1 pint cherry tomatoes
Add to casserole, mixing gently.

5 Add;
¾ teaspoon salt
¼ teaspoon pepper
2 teaspoons fresh chopped basil (½ teaspoon dried)
1 28-ounce can tomatoes in purée, chopped
¾ cup cheese croutons
2 tablespoons grated Parmesan cheese

6 Bake in preheated oven for 45 minutes. For faster cooking, bring to a boil on the stove; then bake for ½ hour.

MUSHROOM SALAD

1 Toss in plastic bag until coated:
   1 pound fresh mushrooms, thinly sliced
   3 tablespoons fresh lemon juice
   Grated rind from 1 lemon

2 Add and toss again:
   ¼ cup thinly sliced leeks
   3 tablespoons Red Wine Vinegar and Oil Dressing (page 162)
   ½ teaspoon salt

3 Marinate in refrigerator for 2 hours.

4 Serve on bibb lettuce sprinkled with:
   ½ teaspoon dill weed
   Lemon pepper

*To use mushrooms as hors d'oeuvre, leave whole.

7

pollo 'n' pasta

PASTA PRIMAVERA
ITALIAN ANCHOVY SALAD

Serves 6

PASTA PRIMAVERA

1 Place in plastic bag:
   2 pounds chicken breasts; skinned, boned, and cut into finger-sized, strips

2 Sauté for 3 minutes:
   ½ cup sliced scallions, using only the denser white, not the green leafy part.
   in:
   2 tablespoons olive oil

3 Add and sauté 1 minute longer:
   2 large cloves garlic, finely chopped

4 Stir in:
   1 cup dry white wine
   2 teaspoons chopped fresh basil (½ teaspoon dried)
   ½ teaspoon salt
   ½ teaspoon freshly ground pepper

5 Pour over chicken and marinate in refrigerator ½ hour.

6 Sauté until lightly browned:
   ½ cup pine nuts
   in:
   1 tablespoon butter
   Remove with slotted spoon; set aside.

7 In same skillet, sauté:
   ½ pound mushrooms, sliced
   ½ cup diced red pepper (½")
   adding:
   1 tablespoon butter
   2 tablespoons olive oil
   Remove with slotted spoon; set aside.

8 In same skillet, sauté for 5 minutes:

3 cups peeled, diced, drained tomato
¼ cup chopped fresh parsley

adding:

1 tablespoon butter
¼ teaspoon baking soda

Set aside.

9 Place in boiling salted water and blanch for 2 minutes after water returns to a boil:

1 cup sliced fresh carrots (¼ " slices)
1½ cups fresh broccoli florets
2 cups fresh asparagus (1 " pieces)

For ease in draining, place vegetables in french fry basket for blanching.

10 Remove vegetables from boiling water. Drain and refresh under cold water. Drain thoroughly.

11 Repeat Steps 9 and 10, blanching for just 1 minute:

2 cups snow peas
1 cup frozen tiny peas
1 cup fresh zucchini, cut into ½ " slices

12 Prepare al dente:

¾ pound pasta—fettucini, linguini, or cappelini

Drain and rinse with cold water. Set aside.

13 Remove chicken from marinade, reserving marinade. Sauté chicken quickly, in large skillet, turning often, in:

2 tablespoons butter

14 Add vegetables gently to chicken in large skillet; simmer until heated through.

15 Warm pasta with large amount of boiling water; drain well.

16 Blend with reserved marinade:

1 cup freshly grated Parmesan cheese
¾ cup whipping cream

Heat until slightly thickened. Add pasta and toss to coat. Continue heating until heated through. Season to taste.

17 Mound spaghetti in center of platter and surround with chicken and vegetables.

18 Sprinkle with sautéed pine nuts.

To prepare in advance, follow Steps 2-12, omitting Step 5, and complete when ready to serve.

A paella pan is perfect for this dish. Use starting at Step 16 and serve in it instead of in a platter.

chickchat

A trendy company spread that can be varied in character by your choice of pasta.

ITALIAN ANCHOVY SALAD

1 Prepare in salad bowl:
   8 cups sliced romaine
2 Toss with:
   ½ cup Green Goddess Dressing II (page 167)
3 Garnish with:
   Croutons
   Capers
   Whole anchovies

Spring Chicken

CANNELONI
ROMAINE ROMANO
Serves 8

CANNELONI

Crèpes

1 Place in 4-cup measuring cup:
> **1½ cups flour**
> **½ teaspoon salt**
> **1 teaspoon ground oregano**

Stir with fork to distribute salt and oregano.

2 Stir in with wire whisk, just until blended:
> **6 eggs, lightly beaten**
> **2 tablespoons melted butter or olive oil**

3 Gradually add:
> **1½ cups water or spinach juice (Filling — Step 3,**
> **page 125)**

Stir with wire whisk until lumps are broken up. (Don't overbeat or the crèpes will be tough.) Allow batter to stand at least 1 hour or overnight in refrigerator before baking crèpes. This allows flour to absorb liquid and air bubbles to break.

4 Heat cured crèpe pan or skillet until it is hot enough that a few drops of water sprinkled on surface dance into small beads.* Brush pan with:
> **Melted butter**

5 Pour in enough batter to coat pan very thinly; 2-3 tablespoons for a 6″ pan. Immediately tilt skillet back and forth to spread batter evenly. (If crèpes seem too thick, add a little water.) Pour back any excess batter.

6 Return pan to heat for 1-2 minutes or until lightly browned. (Crèpe will begin to leave sides of pan.)

7 Slide crèpe onto tea towel. When cool the crèpes may be stacked. (This helps soften edges and facilitates folding or rolling.)

* An electric crèpe pan is wonderful for making crèpes. It is well worth the investment. ➡

Béchamel Sauce

1 In top of double boiler, melt:
   2 tablespoons butter

2 Stir in:
   2 tablespoons flour

3 Gradually add:
   2 cups half & half
   Beat with wire whisk until smooth. Heat over boiling water, stirring constantly, until thickened.

4 Add:
   ½ cup grated sharp cheddar cheese
   Stir until blended. Cover with plastic film to prevent skin from forming.

Filling

1 Sauté:
   ½ pound chopped mushrooms
   2 chopped scallions
   in:
   1 tablespoon butter
   Put into mixing bowl.

2 In same skillet, sauté and chop:
   4 chicken livers
   Add to bowl with mushrooms and onions.

3 Prepare according to package directions:
   2 10-ounce packages frozen spinach
   with:
   1 stick cinnamon
   Drain spinach and discard cinnamon stick. (The spinach juice can be used as the liquid for the crèpes.)

4 Add to spinach mixture:
   ½ cup Italian bread crumbs
   ½ cup grated Parmesan cheese
   3 tablespoons chopped fresh parsley (1 tablespoon dried)
   1 teaspoon salt
   ½ teaspoon freshly ground pepper
   A few grinds nutmeg
   ⅛ teaspoon thyme
   2 ounces ham, chopped
   2 cups chicken or turkey breast, chopped
   4 eggs, lightly beaten
   Mix to blend.

5 Preheat oven to 350°.

6 Have ready:
>**3½ cups Marinara Sauce (page 176)**

7 Grease flameproof pan.** Cover bottom of pan with:
>**¾ cup Marinara Sauce**

8 Spread each crêpe with filling, leaving a ½" border all around. (The amount of filling will vary with size of crêpe. About 2 tablespoons should be sufficient.) Roll crêpe into a cylinder.

9 Arrange filled crêpes in prepared pan. Cover with:
>**2¾ cups Marinara Sauce**

10 Top with:
>**Béchamel Sauce (page 126)**

11 Sprinkle with:
>**¾ cup grated Parmesan cheese**

12 Bake in preheated oven 30-45 minutes until hot and bubbling.

** We like to use a large Paella Pan for serving a crowd.

Canneloni may be completely assembled ahead and baked when ready to serve. Cover and refrigerate. If cold when placed in oven, allow extra baking time.

ROMAINE ROMANO

1 In salad bowl, combine:
>**12 cups romaine**
>**3 cups tomatoes; peeled and cut into bite-sized wedges**
>**1 cup sliced red radishes**
>**½ cup snipped chives**

2 Toss with:
>**Italian Dressing (page 162) to coat**

3 Top with:
>**1 cup freshly grated Romano cheese**
>**2 cups cheese or garlic croutons**

The Company Way
At Step 1, add:
>**1 cup canned artichoke hearts; rinsed, drained, and cut into halves**

127

CRÈPES à la REINE
AVOCADO PINEAPPLE AMBROSIA
with FROSTED GRAPES

CRÈPES À LA REINE

1 Prepare, omitting herbs:
    8 Crepes (page 125)

2 Have ready:
    **2 1-pound chicken breasts, cooked (Cooking Chicken
      Breasts, page 186)**
Skin and bone cooled chicken. Split breasts; then pull apart
each half breast horizontally into two slices following natural
splits. This will yield a total of eight pieces.

3 Preheat oven to 350°.

4 Sauté:
    ½ pound mushrooms, sliced
in:
    1 tablespoon butter
Remove from skillet with slotted spoon; reserve juices. Set
aside.

5 Mix reserved mushroom juice with:
    Chicken broth to make ¾ cup

6 Stir in:
    2 tablespoons sherry
    ¾ cup half & half
    ¼ teaspoon freshly ground pepper
    ½ teaspoon salt

7 Bring to a boil and thicken with:
    3 tablespoons instant blend flour

8 Stir in and mix until blended:
    ½ cup shredded aged Swiss cheese (2 ounces)

9 Place a slice of chicken on each crèpe. Top with:
    1-2 stalks cooked asparagus
    1 tablespoon sauce (above)
Fold crèpes and place in greased baking dish.

128

10 Add sautéed mushrooms and any small remaining pieces of chicken to sauce. Stir in:
¼ cup sliced pimiento, well drained
Pour sauce over crêpes.

11 Sprinkle with:
1 tablespoon grated Parmesan cheese

12 Cover crêpes and bake in preheated oven for 20-30 minutes or until heated through.

To prepare in advance, follow recipe through Step 8, omitting Step 3. Cover with plastic wrap and refrigerate. Allow extra time for baking refrigerated crêpes.

AVOCADO PINEAPPLE AMBROSIA

1 Halve, remove seeds, and cut into balls or 1″ cubes:
2 ripe avocados
Reserve shells.

2 Blend:
½ cup Honey Lime Fruit Salad Dressing (page 169)
1 tablespoon sour cream

3 Toss dressing and avocado with:
1 cup fresh pineapple chunks
1 cup fresh navel or temple orange slices

4 Put fruit into avocado shells. Garnish with:
3 tablespoons grated coconut
Frosted Grapes (below)

The Company Way
Use freshly shredded coconut.

FROSTED GRAPES

1 Beat until frothy but not stiff:
1 egg white

2 Dip into egg white, coating on all sides:
Small bunches of grapes
Place on wire rack.

3 Sprinkle with:
Verifine Sugar (page 172)
Let stand until dry.

Use as a garnish on salads or platters.

chickchat
A gracious luncheon or brunch with style as well as taste.

CHICKEN CACCIATORE
(PASTA)
MARINATED VEGETABLES ROMANO
Serves 4

CHICKEN CACCIATORE

1 In a lidded flameproof casserole, brown under broiler on all sides:

1 4-pound chicken, cut into serving pieces

Drain off fat.

2 While chicken is browning, sauté until wilted:

¼ cup chopped green pepper
½ cup chopped carrots
½ cup chopped celery
1 cup chopped frozen onion (¾ cup fresh)
1 clove garlic, chopped

in:

2 tablespoons olive oil

Add sautéed vegetables to chicken.

3 Stir in:

1 small bay leaf
1 teaspoon salt
¼ teaspoon freshly ground pepper
⅛ teaspoon thyme
¼ teaspoon marjoram
2 tablespoons chopped fresh parsley (2 teaspoons dried)
1 tablespoon chopped fresh basil (1 teaspoon dried)
½ cup dry white wine
4 cups Italian peeled tomatoes in tomato purée, chopped a little

Cover and simmer for 1¼ hours, stirring occasionally.

4 Sauté:

  ½ pound fresh mushrooms, sliced
in:

  1 tablespoon butter

5 Stir in sautéed mushrooms and:

  ¼ cup Parmesan cheese
Cook uncovered 15 minutes or long enough to concentrate sauce.

6 Remove bay leaf.

Serve with pasta and additional Parmesan cheese.

MARINATED VEGETABLES ROMANO

1 Steam until tender-crisp:

  ½ cup unpeeled zucchini, cut into ¼ " slices
  ½ cup unpeeled summer squash, cut into ¼ " slices
Drain well and place in plastic bag.

2 Add:

  ¼ cup Garbanzo beans
  2 tablespoons Italian Dressing (page 162)
Turn bag to coat vegetables with dressing. Marinate overnight in refrigerator, turning occasionally.

3 When ready to serve, toss:

  4 cups sliced romaine
  3 tablespoons corn relish
  2-3 tablespoons Italian Dressing

4 Top with marinated vegetables. Sprinkle with:

  ⅓ cup shredded fresh Romano cheese
  (2 tablespoons dry)

Hatch It Job

CHICKEN SPAGHETTI
MIXED VEGETABLES DIJON
Serves 4

CHICKEN SPAGHETTI

1 Sauté until mushrooms give up their juice (about 5 minutes):
>**1 pound mushrooms, sliced**
>**½ cup frozen chopped onion (⅓ cup fresh)**
>**1 large or 2 small cloves garlic, minced**

in:
>**1 tablespoon butter**

2 Add and simmer until evaporated:
>**⅔ cup dry white wine**

3 Sprinkle with:
>**1 teaspoon chili powder**
>**1 tablespoon chopped fresh basil (1 teaspoon dried)**
>**½ teaspoon freshly ground pepper**
>**½ teaspoon celery salt**
>**½ teaspoon sugar**

4 Stir in:
>**2 15-ounce cans tomato sauce**
>**1½ cups chicken broth**
>**3 cups cooked chicken, cut into strips**
>**½ cup pimiento, sliced in strips**

Bring to a boil, reduce heat and simmer 15 minutes.

5 Stir in:
>**½ cup sliced black olives**
>**1 cup (4 ounces) grated sharp cheddar**

6 Prepare al dente:
>**½ pound vermicelli or cappelini**

7 Toss spaghetti and sauce.

May be mixed ahead, placed in casserole and heated in 325° oven.

Sautéed chicken livers may be used in place of chicken or in additon to chicken. Trim carefully to remove any green spots.

MIXED VEGETABLES DIJON

1 Toss together:

> **4 cups romaine, cut into bite-sized pieces**
> **½ cup shredded carrots**
> **1 cup snap pea pods, stems and strings removed**
> **½ cup chopped raw cauliflower**
> **2 tablespoons snipped chives**
> **Dijon Dressing (page 162)**

2 Garnish with:

> **1½ cups quartered tomatoes**
> **½ cup garlic croutons**
> **¼ cup alfalfa sprouts**

chickchat

Great menu for late night suppers. Everything can be prepared in advance.

Chick-up

your chickchat

8

hen party

WORLD'S BEST CHICKEN SALAD
TOMATO ASPIC
RYE MUFFINS
Serves 10-12

WORLD'S BEST CHICKEN SALAD

1 Remove from bones and tear into 1" x ½" chunks:
  6 pounds cooked chicken breasts (Cooking Chicken Breasts, (page 186)

2 Place in bowl or bag and pour over chicken, shaking to coat:
  ⅓ cup Red Wine Vinegar and Oil Dressing (page 162)
  Leave at room temperature for 1 hour.

3 Mix together:
  ¾ cup mayonnaise
  ¾ cup sour cream
  1 teaspoon salt
  ¼ teaspoon freshly ground pepper

4 Add to dressing:
  2 cups chopped celery
  6 chopped hard-boiled eggs

5 Pour dressing over chicken and stir gently to avoid breaking chicken.

6 Chill in covered bowl before serving.

7 Sprinkle with:
  Toasted slivered almonds

If you are adding fruit to your chicken salad, try substituting equal parts of lemon juice and Raspberry Vinegar (page 174) for red wine vinegar in the dressing.

TOMATO ASPIC

1 Mix together to soften gelatin:
  2 tablespoons lemon juice
  1 envelope unflavored gelatin

2 Bring to boil and remove from heat:
  1 1/3 cups seasoned tomato juice cocktail

3 Dissolve in tomato juice the softened gelatin and:
  1 small package lemon gelatin

4 Add to gelatin mixture:
  2 cups seasoned tomato juice cocktail (cold)
  Chill in refrigerator until gelatin has syrupy consistency.

5 Grease a 6-cup ring mold lightly with:
  Vegetable oil

6 Mix, stirring gently to prevent breaking:
  1 3 1/2-ounce jar caviar, drained
  1/2 cup gelatin mixture
  Pour into prepared mold and place in refrigerator for 5 minutes.

7 Mix each of the following with 1/2 cup gelatin mixture:
  1/2 cup chopped green olives with pimientos
  1 cup sliced hearts of palm
  1 14-ounce can artichoke hearts, halved or quartered

8 Pour olive mixture over caviar in mold. Return to refrigerator for 5 minutes.

9 Repeat with hearts of palm and then artichoke mixture. Finally, pour on remaining gelatin.

10 Chill overnight, covered with plastic wrap until firm. Unmold on a chilled platter.

If you are in a hurry, mix olives, artichokes and hearts of palm with remaining gelatin and pour slowly over caviar, to prevent breaking caviar layer. It will be just as delicious.

137

RYE MUFFINS   *Makes 14 muffins*

1 Preheat oven to 400°.

2 Sift twice, first onto waxed paper; then into an 8-cup measure:
   ⅔ cup all purpose flour
   1⅓ cups rye flour
   ½ teaspoon salt
   2 teaspoons baking powder
   ½ teaspoon baking soda

3 Stir into dry ingredients:
   2 tablespoons caraway seed

4 Beat well in a 2-cup measure:
   2 eggs
   3 tablespoons molasses
   3 tablespoons melted butter or oil

5 Add to liquid ingredients, blending well:
   1 cup buttermilk

6 Add liquid ingredients to dry, blending with a few quick strokes of a rubber scraper. There will still be some lumps. Fill buttered muffin tins ⅔ full, placing ½" water in unfilled muffin cups. Bake in preheated oven 15-20 minutes. After baking, leave muffins in tins for 3 minutes; then remove. Serve immediately or place on wire racks.

Muffins can be prepared ahead through Step 5; combine liquid and dry ingredients and bake just before serving.
To reheat, wrap in aluminum foil and warm at 450° for 5 minutes.
Muffins may be frozen. Allow extra time for reheating.

Unused rye flour should be stored in the freezer.

Chick-in-Salad

SALADE NIÇOISE au POULET

or

PASTA NIÇOISE

SEEDED BREAD STICKS

Serves 6-8

SALADE NIÇOISE au POULET

1 Mix dressing and allow to stand several hours or overnight in refrigerator:

>**1 cup Red Wine Vinegar and Oil Dressing (page 162), made with half olive oil**
>**2 teaspoons Dijon mustard**
>**1 clove garlic, finely chopped or pressed through garlic press**
>**1 teaspoon chopped fresh thyme (¼ teaspoon dried)**
>**½ teaspoon salt**
>**¼ teaspoon freshly ground pepper**

2 Marinate in plastic bag for 2 hours in refrigerator:

>**1 15-ounce can whole Blue Lake string beans, well drained; or 2 cups fresh beans, cooked until tender-crisp**
>**6 artichoke hearts; rinsed, drained, and cut in halves**
>**1½ cups tiny red potatoes, cooked, peeled and cut into ¾" cubes**
>**¾ cup chopped Bermuda or Vidalia onion**
>**4 cups cooked chicken breast, cut into julienne strips**

in:

>**6 tablespoons dressing (Step 1)**

*3 Marinate in another plastic bag for 2 hours in refrigerator:

>**3 cups tomatoes, cut in halves, seeds removed, quartered and drained**
>**2 tablespoons chopped fresh basil**

in:

>**2 tablespoons above dressing**

➡

4 Combine contents of both plastic bags in a large mixing bowl and add:
>   **1½ cups sliced celery**
>   **2-4 tablespoons additional salad dressing to moisten**

Salt and pepper to taste.

5 Place salad on large platter lined with:
>   **3 cups Bibb or Boston lettuce**

6 Garnish with:
>   **12 black olives**
>   **12 stuffed green olives**
>   **12 1″ squares pimiento**
>   **1 2-ounce can rolled anchovies**
>   **12 thinly sliced green pepper rings**
>   **3 hard-boiled eggs, quartered**

* 7 Sprinkle with:
>   **⅓ cup snipped fresh chives**
>   **1 tablespoon snipped fresh tarragon**
>   **1 tablespoon snipped fresh parsley**
>   **Freshly ground pepper**

If fresh herbs are not available, add to dressing:
>   *1 teaspoon dried parsley*
>   *1 teaspoon dried tarragon*
>   *1 teaspoon dried basil*
>   *¼ teaspoon dried thyme*
>   *1 tablespoon dried snipped chives*

Strain dressing before using.

PASTA NIÇOISE

1 Follow recipe for:
>   **Salade Niçoise au Poulet (above)**

2 At Step 2 substitute for potatoes::
>   **1½ cups cooked small elbow macaroni.**

Drain: rinse with cold water, and drain again.

chickchat

This hearty meal-in-one dish, which originated in Nice on the French Riviera, is traditionally made with tuna. We think you'll love it with white meat of chicken.

SEEDED BREAD STICKS

1 Preheat oven to 400°.

2 Brush with melted butter:
Italian style unflavored bread sticks

3 Brush buttered bread sticks with:
Egg white

4 Roll in mixture of:
> **2 tablespoons Parmesan cheese**
> **2 tablespoons sesame seed**
> **2 teaspoons Italian herb seasoning**
> **1 teaspoon kosher salt**

5 Place on ungreased cookie sheets and bake in preheated oven for 10 minutes. Cool on wire rack. Store unused breadsticks in airtight can.

Italian herb seasoning is available in spice departments of most grocers.

OUR NETHERLAND SALAD

1 Blend well with wire whisk:
>**6 tablespoons mayonnaise**
>**½ cup plus 2 tablespoons Red Wine Vinegar and Oil Dressing (page 162)**
>**2 teaspoons Worcestershire sauce**
>**A few grinds pepper**
>**3 tablespoons chopped kosher dill pickles**
>**1 teaspoon chopped chives**

2 Slice into strips ⅛" wide:
>**6 cups crisp iceberg lettuce**
>**1 cup Cooked Chicken Breast (page 186)**
>**1 cup ham, corned beef, or smoked tongue**
>**2 cups tomatoes, Italian plum if available, seeds and pulp removed**
>**1 cup aged Swiss cheese**

3 Toss in salad bowl with:
>**1 teaspoon chopped fresh basil (omit if you can't get fresh)**
>**3 tablespoons snipped fresh chives**
>**1 chopped hard-boiled egg**
>**1 cup sliced hearts of palm**

4 Toss with dressing. Serve promptly after mixing.

To prepare in advance, follow recipe Steps 1 and 2; toss when ready to serve.

APRICOT YEAST MUFFINS

Follow instructions for:
Blueberry Yeast Muffins (page 110)
making the following changes:

1 Soak for 1 hour:
⅔ cup diced dried apricots
in:
¼ cup orange juice
Drain off excess liquid.

2 At Step 4, substitute for milk:
6 tablespoons frozen orange juice concentrate

3 At Step 9, subsitute for blueberries:
Apricots (above)

143

OUR CALIFORNIA COBB SALAD
CORN EBELSKIVER
Serves 4

OUR CALIFORNIA COBB SALAD

1 Remove from bones and finely dice:
    1½ pounds cooked chicken breasts (Cooking
    Chicken Breasts, page 186)

2 In 3-quart salad bowl, toss chicken with:
    8 cups romaine, cut in thin strips
    2 cups tomatoes; peeled, seeded, and diced
    1 cup diced avocado*
    1 tablespoon chopped fresh basil
    ½ cup Red Wine Vinegar and Oil Dressing (page 162)
    Freshly ground pepper

3 Top with:
    8 strips bacon; crisply fried and chopped
    2 hard-boiled eggs, chopped
    ¼ cup snipped fresh chives
    6 tablespoons chopped blue cheese
    ⅔ cup chopped raw cauliflower
Have the pepper mill handy for those who like a lot.

*Sprinkle avocado with lemon juice if you are preparing the salad
ingredients ahead.

*All ingredients can be prepared in advance. Refrigerate each item
in a plastic sandwich bag.*

CORN EBLESKIVER

1 Beat together until stiff:
>**2 eggs**
>**½ teaspoon salt**
>**2 teaspoons baking powder**

2 Add, a tablespoon at a time:
>**3 tablespoons sugar**
>**(½ teaspoon baking soda if using buttermilk in**
>**Step 4)**

Continue beating for 3 minutes.

3 Mix in another bowl:
>**1 ⅓ cups sifted all-purpose flour**
>**⅔ cup corn meal**

4 Stir into flour mixture:
>**3 tablespoons oil**
>**⅔ cup milk or buttermilk**
>**1 cup canned cream-style corn**

Fold in egg mixture.

5 Heat Ebleskiver pan on medium heat. Grease each well with oil and then place in each:
>**½ teaspoon butter**

6 Fill ⅞ full with batter. Cook until bubbly, about 5 minutes. Turn carefully with fork or metal knitting needle and finish baking on other side, about 5 minutes.

7 Continue cooking until all batter is used. Wipe pans with paper towels and grease for second batch.

8 Serve with:
>**Butter**
>**Honey Butter (page 148)**

To make cornbread instead of Ebelskiver, fill greased, heated muffin tins or cornstick pans ⅔ full and bake in preheated 425° oven, 15 minutes for cornsticks or 20-25 minutes for muffins.

JELLIED CHICKEN in ASPIC
DILLED CUCUMBERS
TOMATOES in GUACAMOLE
SALMON SAUCE
STRAWBERRY MUFFINS
HONEY BUTTER
Serves 4

JELLIED CHICKEN in ASPIC

1 Preheat oven to 325°.

2 Have at room temperature:
 10½-ounce can concentrated consommé with gelatin added

3 Season:
 2 whole chicken breasts
 with:
 Seasoned Salt (page 172)

4 Shake in cooking bag:
 1 tablespoon flour

5 Place chicken breasts in bag; close with twister. Place in 2" deep baking pan. Cut six ½" slits in top of bag.

6 Bake 1 hour in preheated oven.

7 Remove from oven and let chicken cool in bag for 15 minutes.

8 Cut off a corner of the bag and drain chicken broth into a small saucepan. Chill broth in freezer until fat hardens; remove fat.

9 Heat broth to melt; pour through strainer into 2-cup measure. Add enough chicken consommé to make 1½ cups.

10 Cover the bottom of an attractive 12" x 12" serving platter with half the consommé. Place in freezer until just set, but not frozen.

11 Skin and bone cooled chicken. Split breasts; then pull apart each half breast horizontally into two slices following natural splits. This will yield a total of eight pieces. Lay chicken slices neatly into the consommé.

12 Surround chicken in attractive design with:
 7-ounce can hearts of palm, split lengthwise into ¼" strips
 1 large whole pimiento, cut into strips
 (If consommé has softened, return to refrigerator to set.)

146

13 Pour remaining consommé over chicken and vegetables. Refrigerate, covered with plastic wrap, several hours or overnight.

14 Serve with:
>   **Salmon Sauce (below)**
>   **Dilled Cucumbers (page 94) (Cube cucumbers at Step 1)**
>   **Tomatoes in Guacamole (page 169)**

SALMON SAUCE

1 Chop in food processor with steel knife:
>   **6½-ounce can red salmon; drained, skin and bones removed**
>   **1 shallot, cut into quarters**
>   **2 tablespoons lemon juice**
>   **½ cup sour cream**
>   **1 cup mayonnaise**
>   **½ teaspoon paprika**
>   **3 anchovies**
>   **2 teaspoons dill weed**

2 Chill before serving.

STRAWBERRY MUFFINS

Makes 8-10 muffins

1 Preheat oven to 400°.

2 Sift twice, first onto waxed paper, then into an 8-cup measure or bowl:
>   **1¾ cups flour**
>   **¼ cup sugar**
>   **¾ teaspoon salt**
>   **2 teaspoons baking powder**
>   **¼ teaspoon baking soda**

3 Beat well in a 2-cup measure:
>   **2 eggs**
>   **½ cup melted butter or oil**
>   **1 teaspoon vanilla**

4 Add to liquid ingredients, blending well:
>   **1⅓ cups finely chopped strawberries***

5 Add liquid ingredients to dry. Stir in with a few quick strokes of a rubber scraper. There will still be some lumps.

*It takes about 2 cups whole strawberries to make 1⅓ cups chopped.

147

6 Fill buttered muffin tins ⅔ full, placing ½" water in unfilled cups. Sprinkle each muffin with:
   1 teaspoon Streusel (page 174)

7 Bake in preheated oven 20-25 minutes.

8 After baking, leave muffins in tins for 3 minutes; then remove and serve immediately or place on wire racks to cool.

Steps 2-4 can be done in advance. At the last minute, combine liquid and dry ingredients, and bake just before serving.

To reheat, wrap in aluminum foil and warm at 450° for 5 minutes, or if frozen, 10 minutes.

HONEY BUTTER

1 Beat until creamy:
   ½ pound unsalted butter, at room temperature

2 Slowly add:
   4 tablespoons honey
   beating until light and fluffy.

3 Store in covered jar in refrigerator.

Serve at room temperature.

chickchat
A perfect luncheon for a hot summer day; add Broccoli Corn Pudding (page 91) to the menu and it becomes a Summer Buffet.

Cold Chicken

GUACAMOLE PITA
or
PITA CLUB
SWEET and SOUR BROCCOLI
Serves 4

GUACAMOLE PITA

1 Toss:
    ½ cup Guacamole Dressing (page 169)
    4 strips bacon, fried and crumbled
    1 cup cubed tomatoes, seeds and juice discarded
    2 cups shredded lettuce

2 Slice in half and open:
    2 pita breads

3 Prepare:
    4 (½ ") slices chicken breast
    4 thin slices ham
Place one slice of chicken and one slice of ham in each pita.

4 Stuff pitas with guacamole salad.

5 Top with:
    Alfalfa sprouts

PITA CLUB

1 Slice in half and open:
    2 pita breads

2 Prepare:
    4 (½ ") slices chicken breast
    4 thin slices aged Swiss cheese
    8 strips crisp bacon

3 Toss:
    2 cups shredded lettuce
with:
    Thousand Island Dressing (page 168)
Divide between 4 sandwiches.

4 Pass extra dressing.

149

SWEET and SOUR BROCCOLI

1 Prepare:
>**1 pound fresh broccoli**

as follows: remove florets and cut stems into ⅛ " diagonal slices. Place florets and stems in plastic bag.

2 Mix and pour over broccoli:
>**2 teaspoons sugar**
>**1 teaspoon salt**
>**2 tablespoons white vinegar**

Marinate overnight in refrigerator.

3 Place in serving dish. Add:
>**2 tablespoons sesame oil**

4 Sprinkle with:
>**Toasted sesame seed**

Refrigerate leftovers in airtight container.

chickchat

Pita recipes created for "planned over" ham and chicken. Keep these in mind for easy company meals on holiday weekends; they also make a casual After-the-Game buffet.

HOT BROWN SANDWICH
VEGGIE PICKLES
Serves 4

HOT BROWN SANDWICH

1 Preheat oven to 500°.

2 In a small saucepan, combine to make BÉCHAMEL SAUCE:
1 cup chicken broth
1 cup milk, half & half, or a combination
3 tablespoons butter
½ teaspoon freshly ground pepper
⅛ teaspoon cayenne pepper
½ teaspoon Worcestershire
2 tablespoons instant blend flour
3 tablespoons finely minced sautéed onion

3 Cook over medium heat, stirring constantly until mixture reaches boiling point and thickens. Remove from heat.

4 Stir in:
8 ounces grated sharp cheddar cheese
Set sauce aside.

5 Toast on one side:
4 slices white bread
Place in four individual au gratin dishes, toasted side down.

6 Cover bread with:
Sliced tomato

7 Cover sliced tomato with:
Sliced chicken breast

8 Cover entire sandwich with:
Béchamel Sauce

9 Sprinkle with:
Paprika
Grated Parmesan

→

10 Bake in preheated oven for 8-10 minutes until heated through and bubbly.

11 Serve immediately.

May be prepared in advance through Step 4. Cover sauce with plastic wrap.

The Company Way
Rinse and drain on paper towels:
> **8 artichoke bottoms**

Place two on each sandwich on top of the chicken breast; then cover with Béchamel Sauce and bake.

chickchat
Our version of a popular, traditional Kentucky sandwich. Serve piping hot!

VEGGIE PICKLES *Makes 1 quart*

1 Boil for 4 minutes:
> **½ cup water**
> **¾ cup Basil Vinegar (page 174)**
> **or ¾ cup red wine vinegar plus 1 teaspoon basil**
> **⅓ cup sugar**
> **2 teaspoons pickling spices**
> **1 teaspoon salt**
> **⅛ teaspoon alum**
> **2 cups sliced Vidalia or sweet onions**
> **3 bay leaves**

Cool.

2 Slice into ¾" slices without peeling, to make 4 cups:
> **Gourmet cucumbers, zucchini, summer squash or a combination**

3 Place vegetables in plastic bag. Pour over them the cooled pickling liquid. Close bag and set into a pan in case of leakage. Store in refrigerator for at least three days before serving, turning a few times each day.

4 After three days, store pickles in a glass jar. Shake occasionally to keep pickles moist.

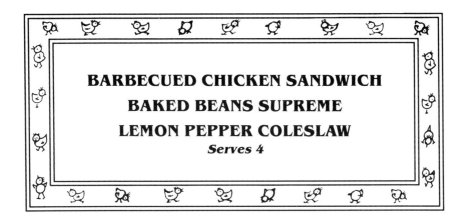

BARBECUED CHICKEN SANDWICH
BAKED BEANS SUPREME
LEMON PEPPER COLESLAW
Serves 4

BARBECUED CHICKEN SANDWICH

1 Prepare:
   1 measure Barbecue Sauce I (page 54)

2 Stir in:
   2½ cups cut-up cooked dark meat of chicken

3 Simmer 10 minutes.

4 Serve with coleslaw on:
   4 toasted hamburger rolls

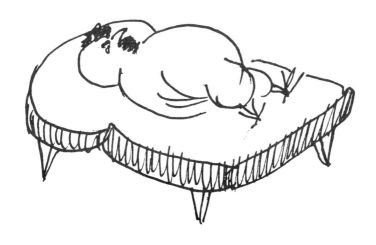

BAKED BEANS SUPREME

1 Preheat oven to 350°.

2 Fry until bacon is crisp:
> ¼ **pound bacon, cut into ¼" strips**
> ¼ **cup frozen chopped onion**

Remove from skillet with slotted spoon.

3 Combine with bacon and onions in a 1-quart flameproof serving dish:
> **1 18-ounce jar baked beans, preferably small pea beans**
> ½ **cup chili sauce**
> **3 tablespoons maple syrup**

4 Bake, uncovered, in preheated oven, for 1 hour.

May be prepared in advance and baked when ready to serve.

This can also be a vegetarian dish. Eliminate the bacon, use meatless baked beans, and sauté the onions in oil.

chickchat

A treasured old Rosenberg family "fix-up," we think you'll agree that these are the best baked beans you've ever eaten. People like them so well that one recipe may not be enough for four hungry people!

LEMON PEPPER COLESLAW

1 Blend with wire whisk:
> ½ **cup mayonnaise**
> **3 tablespoons lemon juice**
> **1 teaspoon lemon pepper**

2 Toss with:
> **1 pound shredded cabbage**

Cover and refrigerate 2 hours or more.

3 Toss again before serving.

This coleslaw will keep in the refrigerator at least 5 days.

9

Friar

sinful and decadent fried chicken

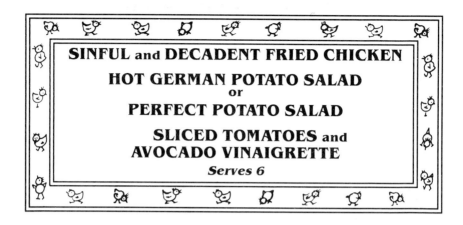

SINFUL and DECADENT FRIED CHICKEN
HOT GERMAN POTATO SALAD
or
PERFECT POTATO SALAD
SLICED TOMATOES and
AVOCADO VINAIGRETTE
Serves 6

SINFUL and DECADENT FRIED CHICKEN

1 Mix in large plastic bag:
> **½ cup corn meal**
> **½ cup flour**
> **1 teaspoon Seasoned Salt (page 172)**

2 Shake in cornmeal mixture, 3 pieces at a time, to coat:
> **2 3-4 pound fryers, cut into serving pieces**

3 In 12″ nonstick or cast iron skillet, heat to bubbling:
> **1 cup chicken fat (page 173)**
> **⅔ cup ham or bacon fat**

4 Fry chicken in fat over medium-high heat, turning every 7 minutes until cooked through, approximately ½ hour. (Add more fat as needed.)

5 Drain chicken on paper towels before serving.

Scrumptious served hot or cold!

chickchat
Now that you really *have* succeeded with chicken without even frying, FRY, FRY AGAIN!!! Kiss your diet goodbye and enjoy!

156

HOT GERMAN POTATO SALAD

1 Boil until tender;
    2½ pounds red potatoes
    Peel and slice.

2 Season with:
    Salt
    Freshly ground pepper

3 Fry until crisp:
    ½ pound bacon, sliced into ⅜" strips
    Remove with slotted spoon.

4 Sauté in bacon grease:
    ¾ cup frozen chopped onion (⅔ cup fresh)
    Do not drain.*

5 Stir into onions:
    1 tablespoon instant blend flour

6 Bring to a boil:
    ¼ cup sugar
    ¼ cup vinegar
    ¼ cup water
    Add gradually to onions, and simmer until thickened, stirring occasionally.

6 Pour over potatoes and bacon.

*You may wish to pour off ¼ cup of bacon fat.

For best flavor, let stand in the refrigerator overnight and reheat in a 350° oven before serving.

There will be some left over, but it tastes better each time you reheat it!

PERFECT POTATO SALAD

1 Boil until tender:
> **3 pounds red potatoes**

Cool.

2 Peel and cut into 1" cubes.

3 Bring to boil:
> **⅓ cup red wine vinegar**
> **¼ cup butter**
> **½ teaspoon salt**
> **¼ teaspoon freshly ground pepper**

4 Add:
> **⅔ cup chopped Vidalia or Bermuda onions**

Pour over potatoes. Marinate at room temperature 1 hour, stirring occasionally.

5 Add:
> **1½ cups chopped celery**
> **4 hard-boiled eggs, chopped**

6 Mix:
> **¾ cup sour cream**
> **1 cup mayonnaise**
> **¾ teaspoon salt**
> **½ teaspoon freshly ground pepper**

7 Pour over potatoes, mix gently, and add additional seasoning to taste.

Store covered in refrigerator. For best flavor, allow to stand 3-4 hours or overnight before serving.

This may seem like a lot of potato salad for six people, but some way (we don't know how) a rather large portion of it disappears when we "season to taste."

SLICED TOMATOES and AVOCADO VINAIGRETTE

1 Slice:
> **1 ripe avocado**

2 Sprinkle with:
> **1 teaspoon lemon juice**

3 Peel and slice:
> **3 large (6 small) tomatoes**

4 Arrange tomato slices on platter attractively with avocado slices. Pour over all:
> **Vinaigrette Dressing (page 164)**

5 Sprinkle with:
> **Dill weed**

10

salad dressings

For a salad you can crow about, follow these simple rules:

1 The use of olive oil produces superb salad dressing, but for reasons of economy and diet, you may use part or all vegetable oil.

2 Use greens that are clean, dry, and crisp. Wash, dry, and store in refrigerator in a plastic bag or crisper with several sheets of paper toweling in bottom of container.

3 Make sure salad ingredients are cold.

4 Chill serving bowl and salad plates in refrigerator or freezer.

5 Drain canned vegetables on paper towels or in salad spinner before marinating.

6 To skin tomatoes, dip in boiling water for 30 seconds.

7 Place cheeses such as Roquefort, Gorgonzola, and blue cheese in freezer for 20-30 minutes before chopping.

8 Use salad dressing sparingly.

9 Do not mix greens and dressing until you are ready to serve.

10 Add croutons after salad has been mixed, immediately prior to serving.

11 Offer pepper mill to guests to season their own salads.

MIX 'N' MATCH SALADS

You never have to serve the same salad twice! Combine several ingredients from each of the following lists for some truly unique salads.

Main Ingredients	Accents	Garnishes
romaine	kohlrabi	chopped raw cauliflower
head lettuce (Iceberg)	okra	pimiento
Boston lettuce	cucumber	olives, black and green
spinach leaves	snap pea pods	artichokes
escarole	zucchini	chopped egg
endive	celery	anchovies
red cabbage	carrots	corn relish
celery cabbage	peppers, red or green	pickled onions
dandelion greens	onions, red or white	croutons
celery root	scallions	blue cheese
bibb lettuce	radishes, fresh or	Gorgonzola cheese
bok choy	marinated	Roquefort cheese
leaf lettuce	mushrooms	feta cheese
Swiss chard	tomatoes	sunflower seeds
	cherry tomatoes	pine nuts
	asparagus tips, raw or	pumpkin seeds
	cooked	chives
	avocado	capers
	pickled beans	garbanzo beans
	pickled beets, julienne	alfalfa sprouts
	bean sprouts	watercress
	broccoli buds	
	cauliflower, steamed	
	Jerusalem artichokes	
	mandarin oranges	
	oranges, navel or	
	tangelo	
	grapefruit	
	pineapple	
	fennel	
	celery leaves	
	hearts of palm	

RED WINE VINEGAR and OIL DRESSING   *Makes 1 quart*

1 Combine:

> **¾ cup red wine vinegar**
> **¼ cup Tarragon Vinegar (page 174)**
> **3 cups oil***
> **1 tablespoon salt**
> **2 teaspoons freshly ground pepper**

2 Refrigerate in tightly covered jar.

*The more olive oil, the better the flavor.

ITALIAN DRESSING   *Makes 1 cup*

1 Mix:

> **1 cup Red Wine Vinegar and Oil Dressing (above)**
> **1·2 garlic cloves, cut in half**
> **½ teaspoon Italian Herb Seasoning***

2 Store in refrigerator overnight before using.

*Italian Herb Seasoning is available in the spice departments of most grocers.

DIJON DRESSING   *Makes 1 cup*

1 Prepare:

> **1 cup Red Wine Vinegar and Oil Dressing (page 162)**

2 Blend in:

> **2 tablespoons Dijon mustard**

3 Refrigerate in tightly covered jar.

For a different flavor, add:

> **1 tablespoon tomato paste**

PIMIENTO DRESSING   *Makes ½ cup*

1 Combine:

> **½ cup Dijon Dressing (above)**
> **1 2-ounce jar pimiento, drained and chopped**
> **1 tablespoon capers, drained**

2 Refrigerate in tightly covered container.

RASPBERRY VINEGAR DRESSING *Makes 1 cup*

1 Combine:
   ¼ cup Raspberry Vinegar (page 174)
   ½ cup oil
   ¼ walnut oil
   ¾ teaspoon salt
   ¼ teaspoon freshly ground pepper
   1 teaspoon Green Pepper or Dijon mustard
   1 tablespoon lemon juice (optional)
2 Store in refrigerator in tightly covered container.

For Chutney Dressing, add:
   2 tablespoons chopped chutney

PUNGENT CELERY SEED DRESSING   *Makes 1¾ cups*

1 Chop in food processor with steel knife:
   1 shallot (walnut sized)
   1 stalk scraped celery
2 Add and blend well:
   1½ teaspoons freshly ground pepper
   1½ teaspoons salt
   ½ teaspoon sugar
   ¼ cup Basil Vinegar (page 174)
   ¼ cup Garlic Vinegar (page 174)
3 With food processor on, drip in slowly:
   1 cup oil
4 Stir in:
   1½ teaspoons celery seed
5 Refrigerate up to one week in a tightly covered jar.

CHAMPAGNE SALAD DRESSING *Makes 1 cup*

1 Mix:
   ¼ teaspoon freshly ground pepper
   ½ teaspoon salt
   2 tablespoons Basil Vinegar (page 174)
   1 tablespoon lemon juice
   ⅓ cup oil
2 When ready to serve, add:
   ½ cup iced champagne
3 Store leftover dressing in tightly covered container in
   refrigerator.

VINAIGRETTE DRESSING I

Makes 1⅓ cups

1 Place in food processor and blend with steel knife until vegetables are finely chopped:

1 large bud hot dill cauliflower
2 tablespoons dill relish, well drained
2 tablespoons sweet pickle relish, well drained
1 tablespoon Dijon mustard
  or 1 tablespoon Mustard with
  Green Herbs
¾ teaspoon salt
½ teaspoon freshly ground pepper
1 tablespoon Garlic Vinegar (page 174)
1 tablespoon Tarragon Vinegar (page 174)
2 tablespoons red wine vinegar

2 With food processor on, pour in a fine stream:

¾ cup oil

3 Refrigerate in tightly covered container.

VINAIGRETTE DRESSING II

Makes 1½ cups

1 Mix:

¾ teaspoon salt
½ teaspoon freshly ground pepper
½ cup chopped fresh parsley
1 tablespoon chopped green onion tops
  or chives
1 tablespoon chopped capers
1 tablespoon chopped dill pickle
1 tablespoon chopped green olives
1 tablespoon chopped green pepper
1 tablespoon chopped pimiento
3 tablespoons red wine vinegar
  or part Garlic Vinegar (page 174)
1 tablespoon Tarragon Vinegar (page 174)
¾ cup olive oil
  or part vegetable oil

2 Store in refrigerator in tightly covered jar.

164

AVOCADO VINAIGRETTE DRESSING   *Makes 1 cup*

1 In bowl of food processor, chop with steel knife:
- **⅓ cup very ripe avocado**
- **1 bud pickled cauliflower**
- **1 teaspoon Dijon mustard**
- **1 tablespoon dill relish or chopped dill pickle**
- **1 tablespoon sweet relish**
- **2 tablespoons pimiento**
- **1 tablespoon red wine vinegar**
- **2 tablespoons Basil Vinegar (page 174)**
- **½ teaspoon salt**
- **¼ teaspoon freshly ground pepper**

2 Add in slow, steady stream with food processor running:
- **⅓ cup oil**

3 Refrigerate in tightly covered jar.

CUCUMBER DRESSING   *Makes 2½ cups*

1 In bowl of food processor chop with steel blade:
- **1½ cups sliced cucumber**
- **1 cup sour cream**
- **2 tablespoons mayonnaise**
- **¼ cup half & half cereal milk**
- **½ teaspoon curry powder**
- **1 teaspoon Dijon mustard**
- **1 teaspoon Worcestershire sauce**
- **1 teaspoon A-1 Steak Sauce**
- **1 teaspoon horseradish**
- **1 small clove garlic, crushed in garlic press**
- **2 dashes tabasco**
- **½ teaspoon salt**
- **¼ teaspoon freshly ground pepper**

2 Refrigerate in tightly covered jar not more than 3-4 days.

SOUR CREAM DRESSING   *Makes 1 cup*

1 Mix together:
- **1 cup sour cream**
- **2 tablespoons lemon juice**
- **2 teaspoons sugar**
- **½ teaspoon freshly ground pepper**
- **¾ teaspoon salt**

2 Refrigerate in tightly covered container.

ROQUEFORT or BLUE CHEESE DRESSING   *Makes 1⅔ cups*

1 Combine:
   1 cup Red Wine Vinegar and Oil Dressing (page 162)
   ⅓ cup mayonnaise
2 Stir in:
   ⅓ cup chopped Roquefort or blue cheese*
3 Store in refrigerator in tightly covered container.

SOUR CREAM ROQUEFORT DRESSING   *Makes 2½ cups*

1 Combine with wire whisk:
   2 cups mayonnaise
   1 cup sour cream
   1 tablespoon Garlic Vinegar (page 174)
   2 tablespoons Basil Vinegar (page 174)
   2 tablespoons red wine vinegar
   2 tablespoons fresh lemon juice
   ½ teaspoon lemon pepper
2 Stir in:
   6 ounces Roquefort or blue cheese, chopped*
3 Store in refrigerator in tightly covered container.

GORGONZOLA CHEESE DRESSING   *Makes 1 cup*

1 Mix with wire whisk or in food processor:
   3 tablespoons lemon juice
   1½ teaspoons Worcestershire sauce
   1 teaspoon Dijon mustard
   1 teaspoon salt
   ¼ teaspoon paprika
   ½ teaspoon freshly ground pepper
   3 tablespoons olive oil
   3 tablespoons oil
2 Stir in:
   3 ounces Gorgonzola cheese, chopped*
3 Store in refrigerator in tightly covered container.

*Chill cheese in freezer for 20 minutes before chopping.

GREEN GODDESS SALAD DRESSING I   *Makes 2 cups*

1 Blend in food processor for 20 seconds:
> **1 cup mayonnaise**
> **½ cup sour cream**
> **3 tablespoons Tarragon Vinegar (page 174)**
> **1 tablespoon chives**
> **3 tablespoons minced onion**
> **⅓ cup chopped fresh parsley (2 tablespoons dried)**
> **1 tablespoon lemon juice**
> **3 anchovies**
> **⅛ teaspoon salt**
> **¼ teaspoon pepper**
> **½ clove garlic**

2 Refrigerate for several hours to allow flavors to blend.

3 To store, refrigerate in tightly covered container.

GREEN GODDESS DRESSING II   *Makes 2 cups*

1 Blend in food processor until smooth:
> **1 2-ounce can anchovies, including oil**
> **¾ cup red wine vinegar**
> **½ teaspoon Worcestershire sauce**
> **3 tablespoons fresh snipped chives (1 tablespoon dried)**
> **3 tablespoons chopped fresh parsley (1 tablespoon dried)**
> **½ teaspoon salt**
> **½ teaspoon celery salt**
> **1 teaspoon Dijon mustard**
> **½ teaspoon freshly ground pepper**
> **¼ teaspoon sugar**
> **1 clove garlic**

2 With food processor ON, add in a slow steady stream:
> **1 cup oil**

3 Refrigerate in tightly covered container.

FRENCH DRESSING

Makes 2 cups

1 Blend well:

⅓ cup sugar
¼ teaspoon freshly ground pepper
1 teaspoon salt
½ cup chili sauce
¾ cup oil
¼ cup red wine vinegar
1 tablespoon Tarragon Vinegar (page 174)
1 tablespoon Garlic Vinegar (page 174)
1 tablespoon water
1 tablespoon grated sweet onion

2 Refrigerate in a tightly covered jar.

THOUSAND ISLAND DRESSING

Makes 1 cup

1 Combine:

½ cup mayonnaise
½ cup chili sauce
2 tablespoons pickle relish
2 tablespoons chopped pimiento
2 teaspoons chopped green pepper
2 teaspoons chopped celery
1 chopped hard-boiled egg
1 teaspoon prepared mustard
1 teaspoon Worcestershire sauce

2 Refrigerate in tightly covered container.

The Company Way
Add:

2 tablespoons black caviar

RÉMOULADE DRESSING

Makes ½ cup

1 Blend:

2 tablespoons Dijon or Green Pepper mustard
2½ tablespoons olive oil
3 tablespoons sour cream
1 tablespoon lemon juice
¼ teaspoon salt
Few grinds fresh pepper
Dash tabasco
1 teaspoon chopped fresh parsley

2 Allow to stand for 3 hours in refrigerator to blend flavors before serving.

3 To store, refrigerate in tightly covered container.

GUACAMOLE DRESSING   *Makes 1½ cups*

1 Chop in food processor with steel knife, using ON/OFF pulses:
   1 shallot (walnut-sized)

2 Add and process:
   1 ripe medium avocado

3 Add and process until smooth:
   ½ teaspoon salt
   ½ teaspoon freshly ground pepper
   ¼ teaspoon paprika
   ¼ cup Basil Vinegar (page 174)
   1 teaspoon prepared Mustard with Green Herbs
      or 1 teaspoon Dijon mustard
   2 teaspoons lemon juice

4 Drip slowly through feed tube with processor ON:
   ½ cup oil

5 Add, using three quick ON/OFF pulses:
   ¼ cup mayonnaise
   1 teaspoon dill weed

6 Refrigerate in tightly covered jar.

FRUIT SALAD DRESSING   *Makes 1⅓ cups*

1 Combine:
   1 cup Red Wine Vinegar and Oil Dressing (page 162)
   3 tablespoons grated sharp cheddar cheese
   3 tablespoons grated pineapple (fresh or canned)
   1 tablespoon honey

2 Refrigerate in tightly covered jar.

This is a nice way to use up a little piece of leftover cheddar.

HONEY LIME FRUIT SALAD DRESSING

Makes 1¾ cups

1 Blend in food processor with steel blade, using two ON/OFF pulses:
   A pinch of ground ginger
   ¼ teaspoon salt
   ¼ cup honey
   ½ cup lime juice

2 With food processor ON, add in a slow steady stream:
   1 cup oil

3 Pour into a jar and add:
   1 teaspoon celery seed

4 Store in refrigerator.

your chickchat

11

nest eggs

When you have the basics at your fingertips,
you're ready to fly through any recipe!

SEASONED SALT
Makes 1 cup

1 Process in food processor with steel knife until pulverized:
1 tablespoon dried celery leaves
1 tablespoon dried chives
2 teaspoons dried parsley
¼ cup salt
1 tablespoon paprika
1½ teaspoons white pepper
¼ teaspoon garlic salt

2 Add:
¾ cup salt
Blend with two ON/OFF pulses.

Prepare in large quantities and give to your friends for hostess gifts.

LOW SODIUM SEASONED SALT

1 Follow instructions for Seasoned Salt. Substitute:
A pinch of garlic powder for garlic salt
Salt substitute for the salt (follow instructions on box for equivalent quantity)

You may prefer to add this seasoning after the food is cooked. Directions on your brand of salt substitute should clarify this.

VERIFINE SUGAR

1 Process in food processor with steel knife for 2 minutes:
Granulated sugar

2 Store in airtight jar.

CINNAMON SUGAR
Makes 1 cup

1 Place in jar and shake to blend:
1 cup sugar
2 tablespoons cinnamon

CHICKEN BROTH

1 Place in 8-quart pot:
5 pounds chicken backs and necks
Water to cover
1 teaspoon salt
2 tablespoons chopped onion
½ cup celery leaves

2 Simmer 2-3 hours.

3 Strain broth; season to taste.

4 Chill; remove hardened fat.

Freeze for future use.

BAG METHOD of RENDERING CHICKEN FAT

1 Preheat oven to 275°.

2 Wash and drain on paper towels:
Chicken fat

3 Place in cooking bag:
1 tablespoon flour

4 Place chicken fat in bag. Close bag and make six ½" slits in top.

5 Place bag in 2" deep baking pan, a little larger than bag. (The pan must be large enough to contain entire contents of bag in case of leakage.)

6 Bake in preheated oven for 45 minutes, or until fat is melted.

7 Remove from oven and cool to luke warm.

8 Pull corner of bag over edge of pan and snip with scissors. Tip pan and pour fat into jar through a strainer.

9 Store in freezer.

Wash and dry chicken fat each time you buy chicken. Store it in a container in the freezer until convenient to prepare.

CLARIFIED BUTTER

1 Heat in skillet until melted and bubbling:
Butter

2 Chill in refrigerator until hardened.

3 Loosen from container and pour off liquid. Pat solids dry to remove all traces of milk.

4 Store remaining butter in refrigerator or freezer.

For convenience, prepare a pound of butter at a time and freeze it.

HERB VINEGARS

TARRAGON or BASIL VINEGAR

1 Mix in jar:
> **1 quart white wine champagne vinegar***
> **¼ cup fresh basil or tarragon leaves**

2 Cover and allow to stand for 3 weeks; strain and pour into clean bottles. Add a generous sprig of the fresh herb for a pretty touch.

GARLIC VINEGAR

1 Mix in jar:
> **1 quart red or white wine vinegar**
> **4 large garlic cloves, cut in half**

2 Allow to stand for 24 hours; strain and pour into clean bottles.

RASPBERRY VINEGAR

1 Mix in jar:
> **1 pint white wine champagne vinegar***
> **1 quart raspberries, crushed**

2 Allow to stand for 3 days; strain and pour into clean bottles.

* Champagne vinegar is available in gourmet food shops. You may also substitute white wine vinegar.

chickchat

Save your salad dressing, catsup and chili sauce bottles to store the special vinegars. Label, and give an assortment to friends for hostess or holiday gifts.

STREUSEL TOPPING   Makes 1¼ cup

1 Place in bowl of food processor with steel knife:
> **½ cup flour**
> **½ cup brown sugar**
> **½ teaspoon salt**
> **1 teaspoon cinnamon**

Blend with two ON/OFF pulses.

2 Add:
> **¼ cup butter, cut into 4 pieces**

Process for 1 minute.

3 Store in freezer in glass jar.

FREEZING VIDALIA ONIONS

1 Buy these mild, sweet onions in season; chop in food processor or slice into rings.

2 Spread on cookie sheets with a double thickness of waxed paper between layers; freeze.

3 When frozen solid, place in plastic bags.

4 Store in freezer.

FREEZING RED or GREEN PEPPERS

1 Dice or cut into julienne strips.

2 Spread on cookie sheets with a double thickness of waxed paper between layers; freeze.

3 When frozen solid, place in plastic bags.

4 Store in freezer.

FREEZING GRAPES

Take advantage of specials on grapes while they're in season.

1 Wash and dry grapes thoroughly.

2 Spread on cookie sheets in single layers separated by double thicknesses of waxed paper.

3 Freeze until solid.

4 Remove from pans and store in airtight containers.

FROZEN LEMON PEELS

1 Wash and dry squeezed lemon peels.

2 Freeze on waxed paper in a single layer.

3 Repack in plastic bag and store in freezer.

Freezing lemon peel makes it easier to grate the zest, the flavorful yellow of the peel.

FREEZING HERBS FROM THE GARDEN

1 Trim plants frequently to prevent buds from forming.

2 Hose down the day before you plan to cut.

3 Cut when dry.

4 Pick leaves off stems.

5 Chop leaves in food processor, or mince with knife.

6 Pack in freezer container, and spoon out as needed.

ITALIAN BREAD CRUMBS

1 Mix:

    1 cup dry bread crumbs
    3 tablespoons grated Parmesan or Romano cheese
    1 ½ teaspoons thyme
    ¾ teaspoon salt
    ½ teaspoon freshly ground pepper

2 Freeze in tightly covered jar.

MARINARA SAUCE

1 Sauté until wilted:

    ¼ cup chopped green pepper
    ½ cup chopped carrots
    ½ cup chopped celery
    1 cup chopped frozen onion (¾ cup fresh)
    1 clove garlic, chopped

in:

    2 tablespoons olive oil

2 Stir in:

    1 small bay leaf
    1 teaspoon salt
    ¼ teaspoon freshly ground pepper
    ⅛ teaspoon thyme
    ¼ teaspoon marjoram
    2 tablespoons chopped fresh parsley (2 teaspoons dried)
    1 tablespoon chopped fresh basil (1 teaspoon dried)
    ½ cup dry white wine
    4 cups Italian peeled tomatoes in tomato purée, chopped a little

Cover and simmer for 1 ¼ hours, stirring occasionally.

4 Sauté:

    ½ pound fresh mushrooms, sliced

in:

    1 tablespoon butter

5 Stir in sautéed mushrooms and:

    ¼ cup Parmesan cheese

Cook uncovered 15 minutes or long enough to concentrate sauce.

6 Remove bay leaf.

Make in quantity and freeze.

Use the freezer labels on the facing page for labelling staples which you prepare in advance. Recipes appear throughout the book.

BASIL	**CINNAMON SUGAR**	**PARMESAN BREADCRUMBS**	**VIDALIA ONION RINGS**
BASIL VINEGAR	**CLARIFIED BUTTER**	**PARSLEY**	**MARINARA SAUCE**
BARBECUE SAUCE	**DIJON DRESSING**	**RASPBERRY VINEGAR**	
BREAD CRUMBS	**GARLIC VINEGAR**	**RED PEPPER**	
CHICKEN BROTH	**GRAPES**	**RED WINE VINEGAR AND OIL DRESSING**	
CHICKEN FAT	**GREEN PEPPER**	**SEASONED SALT**	
CHIVES	**ITALIAN DRESSING**	**STREUSEL**	
CHOPPED VIDALIA ONION	**LEMON PEEL**	**TARRAGON VINEGAR**	
CHOPPED ONION	**LOW SODIUM SEASONED SALT**	**VERIFINE SUGAR**	

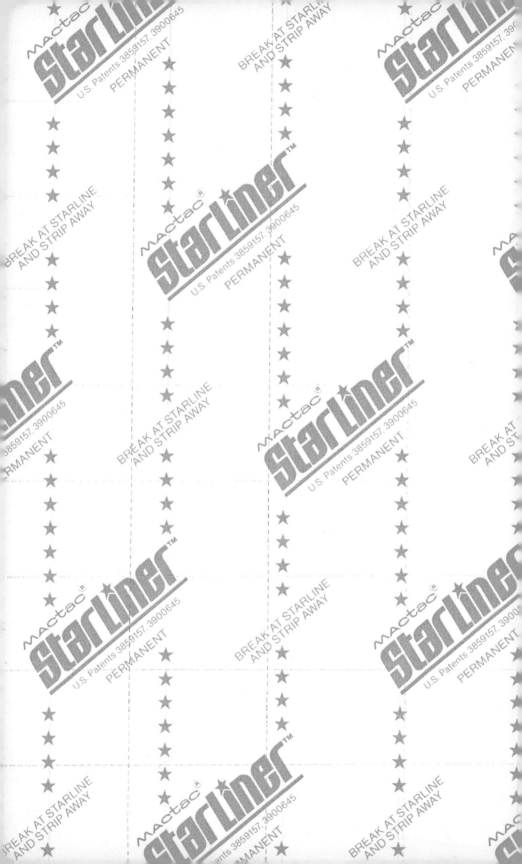

12

chickinformation

ABOUT INGREDIENTS

FLOUR
Recipes refer to presifted all-purpose flour unless otherwise noted. This may be measured without sifting.

For thickening sauces and gravies, our choice is instant blend flour. This is a highly pulverized form of flour that permits quick, lumpfree thickening.

HERBS and SPICES
Recipes specify fresh or dried. In a few instances, only fresh are acceptable. A simple rule of thumb: use three times the amount of fresh in place of dried.

CHOPPED PEPPER or ONION
For convenience we use frozen chopped, either our own or commercially packaged (page 175)

EGGS
Recipes refer to large eggs.

SHORTENING
We prefer butter for flavor. Equivalent amounts of margarine or oil may be substituted. For sautéeing, the amount of shortening can be halved if a non-stick skillet is used. The spray-on preparations may be used according to directions on can.

CHICKEN BASE
A chicken concentrate available in powder or paste; adds flavor to sauces, and can be substituted for chicken broth.

Chick Out Line

178

HOW TO ADAPT OUR RECIPES TO A LOW-CHOLESTEROL DIET

In keeping with the need for lowered fat consumption we frequently accomplish the browning of the chicken skin by broiling, then draining excess fat, rather than the traditional method of frying to add crispness. This actually reduces the total fat consumed, instead of increasing it as in the traditional method. You may further adapt the recipes to a low-cholesterol, low-salt diet by doing the following:

1 Substitute white meat for dark; it is lower in fat.

2 Remove skin from chicken *before* cooking.

3 Remove all surplus fat from chicken *before* cooking.

4 Use salt substitute or **Low Sodium Seasoned Salt (page 172).**

5 To reduce the need for fats and oils, use nonstick cookware.

6 Skim sauces well *before* thickening.

7 In recipes which call for nuts, use walnuts.

8 Replace butter or stick margarine with soft (tub) margarine; the softer the margarine, the lower it is in saturated fats.

9 Replace olive and coconut oil (mono-unsaturated fats) with vegetables oils such as corn, peanut, soy bean, safflower and cottonseed (poly-unsaturated fats).

EQUIPMENT WE LOVE

1 **Flame-proof cookware** is the dream of all those who search for shortcuts! With a little planning, one dish will often suffice to prepare a main course from start to finish. We prefer enamelled cast iron; the cast-iron for even cooking and the enamelled exterior for attractive serving. This cookware has the added convenience of being usable both on the range and in the oven. For recipes in this book, we suggest a large au gratin dish and covered pots in 2-quart and 5-quart sizes.

2 **Boning knife** — Buy the best and keep it sharp.

3 **Flat Bottom Spoon** — The easy way to smooth sauces.

4 **Meat Cleaver** — Indispensable for preparing chicken wings and for chopping bones for the soup pot.

5 **Macerating Mallet** — Use the flat side for pounding chicken breasts.

6 **Food Processor** — Not a must, but a delight!

7 **Salad Spinner** — For draining greens.

8 **Wire Whisk** — For lump-free mixing.

9 **Nonstick Skillets** — For easy clean-up and for decreasing the amount of oil or butter needed for browning or sautéeing. Treat yourself to an 8″ and a 12″.

BUYING CHICKEN

1 Poultry production is an efficient means of converting plant protein to animal protein; less feed is needed per pound of meat produced than for other animal protein. Therefore chicken is a good value.

2 When buying chicken, bear in mind that whole chicken yields only 51% of its weight in meat.

3 Refer to the chart below when comparing the prices of whole chicken and chicken parts:

If the price per pound of whole fryers is—	Chicken parts are an equally good buy if the price per pound is—*					
	Breast half Without rib	With rib	Thigh	Thigh and drumstick	Drumstick	Wing
.49	.67	.65	.55	.53	.50	.39
.51	.70	.67	.57	.55	.53	.41
.53	.72	.70	.59	.57	.55	.43
.55	.75	.73	.61	.59	.57	.44
.57	.78	.75	.63	.61	.59	.46
.59	.80	.78	.66	.63	.61	.48
.61	.83	.81	.68	.66	.63	.49
.63	.86	.83	.70	.68	.65	.51
.65	.89	.86	.72	.70	.67	.52
.67	.91	.89	.75	.72	.69	.54
.69	.94	.91	.77	.74	.71	.56
.71	.97	.94	.79	.76	.73	.57
.73	1.00	.97	.81	.78	.75	.59
.75	1.02	.99	.84	.81	.77	.60
.77	1.05	1.02	.86	.83	.79	.62
.79	1.08	1.04	.88	.85	.81	.64
.81	1.10	1.07	.90	.87	.83	.65
.83	1.13	1.10	.92	.89	.85	.67
.85	1.16	1.12	.95	.91	.87	.69
.87	1.19	1.15	.97	.93	.89	.70
.89	1.21	1.18	.99	.95	.91	.72
.91	1.24	1.20	1.01	.98	.94	.73
.93	1.27	1.23	1.04	1.00	.96	.75
.95	1.30	1.26	1.06	1.02	.98	.77
.97	1.32	1.28	1.08	1.04	1.00	.78
.99	1.35	1.31	1.10	1.06	1.02	.80

* Based on yields of cooked chicken meat with skin (only ½ skin on wings and backs included), from frying chickens, ready to cook, that weighed about 2¾ pounds. Adopted from USDA 1974 Agricultural Yearbook.

CLASS AND GRADE

1 Chickens are classified by age and weight.

> **Young chickens** include:
> Broiler-fryers; 7-9 weeks old; 2-3½ pounds
> Roasters; 15-16 weeks old; 3½-6 pounds
> Capons; surgically desexed males; 16 weeks old; 4-7 pounds
>
> **Mature chickens** are labeled as hens, heavy hens, or stewing chickens. They are approximately 1½ years old and weigh 4½-6 pounds.

2 The younger the chicken, the more tender it will be. Tenderness is not denoted by grade.

3 The more mature the chicken, the more flavor it will have.

4 Before being assigned a grade, chickens are inspected. The USDA inspection mark denotes a healthy bird, processed under sanitary conditions, properly packaged, and accurately labeled. The inspection mark may appear only on the large shipping box, not on individual chickens.

5 After inspection, the chicken is graded as follows:
> Grade A for chickens which are full-fleshed and meaty, and have been well finished.
> Grade B for chickens which are less meaty and less attractively finished.

METHODS OF PACKAGING CHICKEN

1 **Ice pack or CO_2 pack**
Chicken is processed and shipped fresh packed in shaved ice or carbon dioxide "snow."

2 **Deep chill, chill pack, or crystal pack**
Chicken is cooled rapidly to 28-32°F but not frozen. It is then dry-packed and shipped in refrigerated trucks. There may be some crystal formation, but you should be able to depress the flesh with your finger.

3 **Frozen**
Chicken is quick-frozen at the plant. It is then shipped and sold frozen.

STORING CHICKEN IN THE REFRIGERATOR

1 Before refrigerating chicken, unwrap and cover loosely to prevent the formation of anaerobic bacteria which give an offensive odor.

2 Chicken refrigerated in tray packs may have a strong odor; disregard this unless it lingers more than a few minutes after opening package.

3 Chicken should not be stored in market paper.

4 Cut-up chicken can be stored for two days in the coldest part of your refrigerator; whole chicken can be stored three days.

5 Do not let juices from chicken drip on other food.

6 Thoroughly clean all work surfaces which come in contact with raw chicken.

7 Never store partially cooked chicken; always cook completely before refrigerating or freezing.

8 Never store a stuffed chicken. Stuffing can be prepared in advance but must not be put in the chicken until cooking time. After cooking, stuffing must be stored separately.

STORING LEFTOVER CHICKEN

1 Never keep cooked food of any kind at room temperature for more than 4 hours. Chicken prepared in a sauce should not be held at room temperature at all; keep refrigerated until ready to serve.

2 Remove leftover chicken from broth, gravy, or stuffing, and store separately.

3 Cool leftovers quickly by placing them in a shallow pan and refrigerating.

4 Leave wrapping loose when cooling cooked poultry.

5 Reheat leftover broth or gravy to boiling before serving.

FREEZING CHICKEN

1 To freeze chicken parts, rinse and pat dry. Freeze on cookie sheet, separating layers with a double thickness of waxed paper. Bag when frozen solid.

2 To freeze whole chickens, wash inside and out; remove giblets and freeze separately.

3 If desired, freeze wing tips and backs separately for stock. Chop backs into 4 pieces.

4 Freezer bags and containers should be moisture and vapor resistant. Frost-free freezers in particular will dehydrate poorly wrapped foods.

5 Label freezer packages with name of food and date of freezing.

6 Optimum freezer storage times are as follows:
   Commercially frozen chicken: 12 months
   Home frozen chicken: 3-6 months
   Cooked chicken: 2 months

7 Freezer should be 0°F or colder.

8 Freeze chicken rapidly by using the coldest part of your freezer. (Check owner's manual for this information.) Leave 1" airspace on all sides of each package to allow air to circulate.

9 Thaw chicken in refrigerator with wrapping loosened; for faster thawing, place in plastic bag and immerse in cold water.

10 Approximate thawing times in the refrigerator are as follows:
   Whole chicken (4 pounds): 12-16 hours
   Chicken pieces: 4-9 hours

11 Cook chicken promptly after thawing.

12 Do not refreeze raw chicken.

NUTRITION

1 Chicken is an excellent source of protein, vitamins, and minerals; it is low in fat and cholesterol.

2 Refer to the charts below for an exact breakdown.

3 Skin color is irrelevant to nutritional value, flavor, tenderness, or fat content. Color ranges from white to deep yellow, but should never be gray and pasty.

Percentage of RDA Contributed by Chicken Parts
(As Purchased)

With Bone	Vitamin A	Thiamine	Riboflavin	Niacin	Iron	Calcium	Phosphorus	Protein
1 half breast (6 oz.)	2.3	5.7	6.8	67.4	5.6	1.5	23.7	63.0
1 drumstick (4 oz.)	1.4	3.6	7.9	20.7	4.3	.8	11.7	32.5
1 thigh (4 oz.)	2.6	3.7	8.0	24.3	4.9	.9	12.9	34.4
1 wing (2 oz.)	.9	1.0	1.6	9.1	1.6	.4	4.0	12.5
4 oz. livers	466.0	10.4	130.9	52.4	53.9	1.2	30.9	45.3

Nutritive Breakdown By Parts (With Bone)

Chicken parts — with bone (raw, as purchased)	Protein (grams)	Fat (grams)	Calories	Carbohydrates (grams)
1 half breast (6 oz.)	28.4	12.6	234.8	—
1 drumstick (4 oz.)	14.6	6.6	122.0	—
1 thigh (4 oz.)	15.5	13.7	189.2	—
1 wing (2 oz.)	5.6	4.9	68.0	—
4 ozs. livers	20.4	4.4	141.5	3.9

Charts courtesy of Agriculture Handbook No. 8-5, 1979, USDA; Food and Nutrition Board, National Academy of Sciences — National Research Council, 1980.

COOKING CHICKEN BREASTS

BAG METHOD

1 Preheat oven to 325°.

2 Sprinkle chicken breasts with:
   Seasoned Salt (page 172)

3 Place in cooking bag:
   1 tablespoon flour

4 Place chicken breasts in bag and place bag in 2" deep pan.

5 Close bag with twister and cut six ½" slits in top of bag.

6 Bake in preheated oven for 1 hour.

7 Remove from oven and let stand for 15 minutes.

8 Cut off a corner of bag and drain broth into a jar for later use.

STEAMING METHOD

1 Add to water in base of steamer:
   ½ teaspoon chopped dried tarragon
   1 teaspoon dried parsley
   ⅛ teaspoon thyme
   1 small bay leaf
   1 teaspoon celery leaves

2 Place chicken breasts in steamer and season with:
   Salt and freshly ground pepper

3 Bring water to a boil and steam for 30 minutes or until tender. *Strain and save remaining steaming liquid for later use. It's better than any chicken broth you can buy!*

MICROWAVE METHOD

1 Arrange chicken breasts symmetrically on plate.

2 Sprinkle with:
   Seasoned Salt (page 172)

3 Place a sheet of waxed paper over chicken to prevent splattering.

4 Cook at high power (700 watts) 5½-7 minutes per pound.

5 Allow to stand for 5 minutes before checking for doneness; microwaved food continues to cook during standing time.

6 Cook longer if needed.

POACHING METHOD

1 In pot, bring to a boil sufficient water to cover chicken breasts. For each 6 pounds of chicken breasts, add:
   ½ teaspoon salt
   ½ cup chopped celery leaves
   2 tablespoons chopped onion

2 Add chicken breasts; return to a boil.

3 Reduce heat and simmer for 5 minutes.

4 Turn off heat and leave chicken in hot water 15 minutes.

SKINNING AND BONING CHICKEN

1 Chill chicken until very cold before boning.

2 Use your sharpest knife, preferably a boning knife.

3 Skin the whole chicken or whole breast before disjointing and boning.

4 Save leftover bones and skin for stock.

5 Remember, boning chicken yourself is money in your pocket, and it is a skill which you can easily learn!

Quartering A Chicken

1. Place chicken on back and, with sharp knife, cut in half along the breast bone.

2. Pull the two sections apart, breaking the ribs away from the backbone; finish cutting with knife.

3. Take each half and separate the leg-thigh combination from breast-wing portion by cutting between the thigh and the breast.

Cutting Up A Whole Chicken

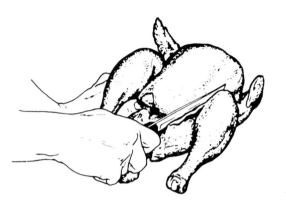

1. Place chicken, breast side up, on cutting board. Cut skin between thighs and body.

2. Grasping one leg in each hand, lift chicken and bend back legs until bones break at hip joints.

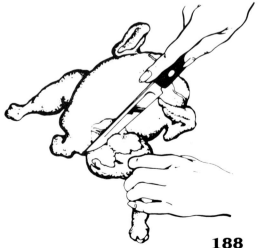

3. Remove leg-thigh from body by cutting (from tail toward shoulder) between the joints, close to bones in back of bird. Repeat other side.

4. To separate thighs and drumsticks, locate knee joint by bending thigh and leg together. With skin side down, cut through joints of each leg.

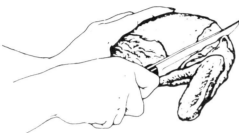

5. With chicken on back, remove wings by cutting inside of wing just over joint. Pull wing away from body, and cut from top down, through joint.

6. Separate breast and back by placing chicken on neck-end or back and cutting (toward board) through joints along each side of rib cage.

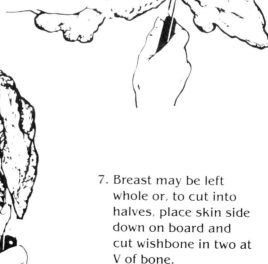

7. Breast may be left whole or, to cut into halves, place skin side down on board and cut wishbone in two at V of bone.

Boning A Whole Chicken Breast

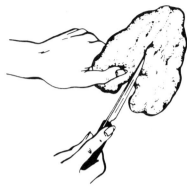

1. Place skin side down on cutting board with widest part nearest you. With point of knife, cut through white cartilage at neck end of keel bone.

2. Pick up breast and bend back, exposing keel bone.

3. Loosen meat from bone by running thumbs around both sides, pull out bone and cartilage.

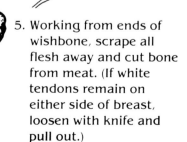

4. Working with one side of breast, insert tip of knife under long rib bone inside thin membrane and cut or pull meat from rib cage. Turn breast and repeat on other side.

5. Working from ends of wishbone, scrape all flesh away and cut bone from meat. (If white tendons remain on either side of breast, loosen with knife and pull out.)

Boning Half A Chicken Breast

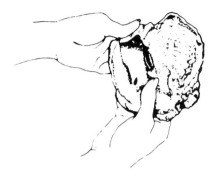

1. Holding breast half in both hands, bend and break keel bone.

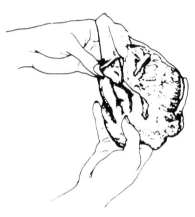

2. Run thumb between meat and keel bone, removing the bone and strip of cartilage.

3. Using both thumbs, loosen meat from rib cage.

4. Pull or scrape breast meat away from bones. (If small piece of pulley bone remains, pull it out or cut away with knife.)

Boning A Chicken Thigh

The moist, flavorful dark meat of thighs makes them a favorite chicken part for many, and when boned, they are even more versatile.

1. Place thigh on cutting board, skin-side down, and cut along thin side, joint to joint.

2. Cut meat from one joint; then pull or scrape meat from bone.

3. Cut meat from opposite joint.

Cutting Wings Into Drumettes

1. With skin side down, flatten wing on cutting board with wingtip on left and thicker (drumette) portion on right.

2. Cut through joint, leaving as much skin as possible on drumette.

Pictures courtesy of the National Broiler Council.

Index

before you use the index, read this!

Index listings are printed as follows:

1 Recipes appear by their titles.

apricot yeast muffins, 143

2 Categories are listed followed by recipes in them.

BREADS
Apricot Yeast Muffins, 143
Blueberry Yeast Muffins, 110

3 Ingredients are listed followed by recipes which include them.

Apple
Bag Roasted Chicken with Harvest Dressing, 100
Baked Applesauce, 40

The following listings are particularly useful in planning meals:

CHICKEN, about
Chicken breast, cooked
PLANNED-OVERS
ONE DISH MEALS
LUNCHEONS AND LIGHT SUPPERS

Chicken recipes are also listed according to the chicken parts they use:

Chicken, breast
Cordon Bleu, 118
Dugléré, 17

194

198

203

Typefaces used in this book are Benguiat and Uncial.

ORDERING INFORMATION

Mail Orders and Checks to: Marlance, Inc.
           1070 Barry Lane
           Cincinnati, OH 45229
           (513) 281-0530

Price: $8.95 plus $1.75 handling
      Ohio residents add 49¢ sales tax
      Outside continental United States add $1.00 per book
      Canadian orders must be paid in U.S. dollars

PLEASE PRINT OR TYPE

Please send ____ copies of HOW TO SUCCEED WITH CHICKEN
                 WITHOUT EVEN FRYING

Name_____

Address_____

City, State_____ Zip_____

Gift card message_____

Enclosed is my check for $_____

PLEASE PRINT OR TYPE

Please send ____ copies of HOW TO SUCCEED WITH CHICKEN
                 WITHOUT EVEN FRYING

Name_____

Address_____

City, State_____ Zip_____

Gift card message_____

Enclosed is my check for $_____

PLEASE PRINT OR TYPE

Please send ____ copies of HOW TO SUCCEED WITH CHICKEN
                 WITHOUT EVEN FRYING

Name_____

Address_____

City, State_____ Zip_____

Gift card message_____

Enclosed is my check for $_____

ORDERING INFORMATION

Mail Orders and Checks to: Marlance, Inc.
1070 Barry Lane
Cincinnati, OH 45229
(513) 281-0530

Price: $8.95 plus $1.75 handling
Ohio residents add 49¢ sales tax
Outside continental United States add $1.00 per book
Canadian orders must be paid in U.S. dollars

PLEASE PRINT OR TYPE

Please send ____ copies of HOW TO SUCCEED WITH CHICKEN
WITHOUT EVEN FRYING

Name_____

Address_____

City, State_____ Zip_____

Gift card message_____

Enclosed is my check for $_____

PLEASE PRINT OR TYPE

Please send ____ copies of HOW TO SUCCEED WITH CHICKEN
WITHOUT EVEN FRYING

Name_____

Address_____

City, State_____ Zip_____

Gift card message_____

Enclosed is my check for $_____

PLEASE PRINT OR TYPE

Please send ____ copies of HOW TO SUCCEED WITH CHICKEN
WITHOUT EVEN FRYING

Name_____

Address_____

City, State_____ Zip_____

Gift card message_____

Enclosed is my check for $_____